# 10 Things Every Woman Needs To Know About Men

## Understand His Mind and Capture His Heart

*By Sabrina Alexis and Eric Charles*

## Copyright Information and Disclaimer

Now let's move on to the fun stuff...

ISBN: 151779109X

ISBN-13: 978-1517791094

*Dedicated to all the amazing ladies
looking for lasting love.*

# Author's Note

You could say I've been working unofficially on this book since a moment in the winter of 2008. After three months of dating the first guy to make my stomach flip in two years, he ghosted. I only found out it was over when he called me by accident, thinking he was calling another girl, and hung up. I was in shock. I won't go into the details here (I broke it all down in the introduction of *He's Not That Complicated*, the first A New Mode book written by me and Eric Charles), but long story short, I got the answers I really needed to hear about what had gone wrong from some guy friends. I was stunned, I was enlightened, and best of all I felt okay. I mentally vowed in that moment to do something one day to help other women feel the way I felt right then: empowered, clearheaded, and, for once, not confused by men. I started by founding A New Mode with Eric and creating a plethora of content devoted to helping women uncover the truth about relationships. But I wanted to do more.

This is the first book I decided to fly solo on. Eric worked closely with me as my trusted advisor and man decoder and provided invaluable insights into the male mind that I never could have uncovered on my own, but I decided to write this in my own way and in my own voice.

This is not a book filled with tricks and gimmicks. There are no strategies to make a man fall in love with you, no formula for approximately how long to wait before responding to his text, no manipulative tactics, no cut-off times for ending a date. I mean, I could write a book promising you all those things, and I'd probably make a lot of money. But I won't, because those things won't lead to a healthy relationship or lasting love, and they won't bring you happiness — and isn't that what we all want at the end of the day?

I was once completely baffled by men, desperately trying to find the answers, picking up the pieces after a string of failed relationships and wondering what I'd done wrong, what I must have missed, how I could have been so clueless. And now it's clear. Now I know. And soon, you will, too.

~ Sabrina

# Introduction

*"Be patient and tough; someday this pain will be useful to you."*

*~ Ovid*

I am alone. It is fall 2006, and I am a senior in college. I should be in class, but I can't bear the thought of going. I can't pretend that everything is normal. I can't hold myself together. The agony rips through me, unrelenting. *How will I ever get through this?*

I reread *Vanity Fair* for the tenth time in two days. Jennifer Aniston is on the cover. She and Brad Pitt have recently divorced, and she is opening up about it for the first time. In the article, she says she gave herself one pity day. One day to cry and feel sorry for herself and mourn the loss of what she'd had. But then she said *no more* and moved forward. That's what I've decided to do. While Jennifer doesn't know it, this article has caused me to feel a bond with her unlike any other, a sisterhood of sorts that surpasses anything I share with an actual friend. She has experienced this awful pain, even worse pain, and she is coming out on the other side. There is hope.

Next on the agenda, I watch the first season of *The O.C.* I need to lose myself in the lives of people whose problems surpass my own. When Luke cheats on Marissa in Tijuana and she overdoses, I find another sister. I feel her fictional pain; I know what it is to want nothing but numbness and escape. I can't fathom ever returning to normalcy again. The pain boxes me in, and there seems to be nothing that exists outside of it.

Feeling slightly less alone thanks to Jen and Marissa, I seek answers. I need to know why. I need to understand how something that started off so right went so terribly wrong. I need to know how two people can love each other and still not make it work. I need to know what I did wrong, what I missed or overlooked. I need to understand... all of it. Why couldn't I make him happy? Why couldn't he commit in a real way, even though he loved me very much? Why did I keep going back to him, even though I knew I deserved better?

It took years for me to get the answers to those questions. The story of that relationship and why it didn't work out is a book in and of itself, a deeply personal story I hope to tell one day. There isn't room to share the entire story here, but bits and pieces of it are here, along with some of the answers I found. You'll also find other personal stories of mine throughout the book revealing what I learned, through much trial and error, in subsequent relationships, as well as guy confessions that provide unique insight into the male mind — straight from the horse's mouth! At the end of each chapter I've included a recap of what was covered in the chapter in the form of bite-sized mantras that you can refer back to while you work on internalizing these concepts. And you'll find exercises at the end of every chapter that I hope will empower you the way they empowered me. I also created a resource page with a selection of related articles for each chapter in case you want more information — Eric and I have been writing content for over six years now, and there was only so much I could squeeze into this book!

My goal in writing this book was twofold: to help you understand men, and to help you understand yourself. (A relationship takes two, after all!)

When you understand a man and can appreciate and embrace his masculine energy, you will bring out the best in him, resulting in an amazing relationship. When you don't understand a man, and instead become jaded or frustrated and adopt an "all men suck" mantra, you will give off a negative energy that will inevitably land you in situations where you suffer, because instead of bringing out

4

the best in him, you will bring out the worst, resulting in a painful relationship.

This book will also teach you quite a bit about yourself. You'll see areas where you need to grow, bad thought patterns that lead you into damaging situations, faulty mindsets that can ruin your relationship, and more. You may also find answers to what went wrong in some of your previous relationships... I certainly did along the way! My mission with this book, and with all the content I write, is to help you learn from my mistakes and to let you know you're not alone. I've been where you are, and you will be okay.

The not knowing used to kill me. The questions and doubts... what did I do wrong? Why is he doing this? Why did he leave? But the answers can be found if you look in the right place; you can understand and you can find peace. You can learn what it takes to have an amazing relationship and what is preventing you from getting one. You can get the love you want. You just need to understand a few things about men first...

# Chapter 1: When a Guy Likes You, It's Obvious

*"Women have a wonderful instinct about things.*
*They can discover everything except the obvious."*

*~ Oscar Wilde*

The number one question we get hit with on A New Mode is some variation of: Does he like me?

I get it, *believe me*. I have asked that same question countless times. I have experienced the pain, frustration, and insecurities that come when a guy arouses those fluttery feelings within you and you don't quite know if he feels it, too. Sometimes it seems like he does... other times you just don't know. And the not knowing eats away at you. So you question, you analyze, you try to "crack his code," you ask your friends, you read articles on "signs he likes you" and try to check off every single one, even if it requires some stretching of the truth and a bit of self-delusion. When he says or does something that indicates he likes you, you're ecstatic. You are brimming with hope and can't help but envision how amazing it will be when everything comes together. When he says or does something that makes you think maybe he doesn't have the same feelings, you're devastated. You wonder if there's something wrong with you, if it was something you said or did. *Was I too desperate? Too needy? Did I not show enough interest? Too much interest? Am I too fat? Too skinny? Too loud? Too quiet? Why doesn't he like me?!*

From personal experience, I can tell you that trying to decipher whether or not a particular guy had feelings for me was a total waste of my time and energy. It wasn't until many, many years had passed that I learned the truth: If you have to ask, you already have your answer.

When boy meets girl and boy likes girl, he makes sure she knows it. And she doesn't even have to ask or wonder because she can just tell. And the people around them know it, too. It's just *obvious*. It's clear as day. There are no mixed messages, no codes to decipher, no hidden meanings to find.

## When You Know the Truth...

When you realize these truths about men, *really* realize them, you will free yourself from a prison of self-doubt and a shaky sense of self-worth. You will live your life in a way that makes you happy, and when a guy comes along you won't stress or strategize. You will continue to be yourself and you will know that if he likes you, he will pursue you. And if he doesn't give you a clear indication that he likes you, then it's because he doesn't, and that's really no big deal.

When you understand how a guy operates when he likes a girl, you will see how useless it is to analyze the signs. You will see that engaging in this futile practice results in nothing more than driving you crazy and eroding your self-esteem. You will get off the endless roller coaster ride of ups and down, highs and lows, and will enjoy the beauty of living life serenely on steady, unshakeable ground.

## Guys Don't Hide Interest

Men, in general, are goal-oriented. They see something they want and they pursue it. It's how they're wired. It goes against a man's nature to like a girl, see an opportunity to pursue her, and turn the other way.

Men don't typically play games or do things to intentionally mislead or manipulate you. When a guy likes you, he is drawn to you. He wants to be around you, he finds reasons to talk to you, he becomes a presence in your life, and he gives you a special kind of attention that no one else is given. He lights up around you, he is excited to see you, he loves spending time with you, and he wants to get to know you more. Once he does, either a relationship will develop, or it won't. (If it doesn't, it's probably because he realized you aren't compatible.)

Men really aren't that complicated. The problem is that we girls make them so. The reason it can seem so complicated and confusing is because when we like a guy, we cling to any glimmer of hope that he feels the same way and focus exclusively on the small things he says or does that hint at any interest, rather than taking in the entire picture. When a guy likes you, there's nothing to look for. It almost seems silly to ask the question because it's just so *obvious*! You just know. When you don't know, that's when you go into emotional detective mode and start looking for evidence that indicates reality is what you want it to be.

## Personal Story

A few years ago, I met a guy who seemed perfect for me in every way (at least on paper). He was funny, outgoing, kind, and successful — not to mention stop-you-in-your-tracks gorgeous. We had mutual friends, so I'd run into him here and there and he was always super flirty. And he would say things that led me to believe my interest was reciprocated... that I was beautiful, cool, great to talk to, stuff like that. It drove me absolutely crazy because it seemed like he liked me, but he wasn't asking me out or even asking for my number.

I knew conventional wisdom would say that he just wasn't into me, but it didn't feel that way! Friends even warned me that that's just how he is, that he flirts with everyone, but I couldn't let go of the notion that I was different, that *this* was different.

I spent many months obsessing over whether or not he liked me. When our paths would cross, he would give me just enough hope to hang onto, but he never attempted to hang out with me on purpose, and all our interactions were the result of coincidentally being in the same vicinity.

I couldn't, for the life of me, figure out why he wasn't just asking me out. My mind would churn out all sorts of possible explanations. Maybe he doesn't think I'm interested in him because I get shy when I talk to him, and he doesn't want to be rejected... maybe he's intimidated by me... maybe he's worried it would be weird because we have a lot of mutual friends... maybe he's just scared because he knows I'm perfect for him and he thinks we'll end up together, and that's frightening for a guy, so he's resisting it. (No, I am not making that last one up, that was an actual, genuine thought in my head!)

One night it was his friend's birthday party and I brought a girlfriend with me. When he saw my friend, I noticed a look in his eye that he'd never had when he looked at me. They started talking, and it was obvious he was super into her.

He got her number and called to ask her out a few days later. Even at that point I *still* clung to a glimmer of hope that he would see the light and want to be with me. As their relationship stretched on, I had to face the facts.

There was never a secret connection. This story I'd concocted of him suppressing his all-consuming feelings for me was absolute fiction. Sure, he liked flirting with me...he just didn't *like* me. When he met a girl he did like, it was obvious to all and he didn't hesitate to make a move.

This guy is now one of my closest friends, and through our friendship I've realized that it never would have worked between us (we're just not a match). The only reason I couldn't see this from the start is because I chose to live in a fantasy. I got completely caught up in trying to figure out how he felt about me and why I wasn't good enough for him.

Over the years I've noticed he is incredibly flirty and charismatic, but that's just his personality. Time and time again I've seen that when he likes a girl, he goes for it without hesitation.

## Why Women Get Confused

*"Love can sometimes be magic. But magic can sometimes… just be an illusion."*

*~ Javan*

If it's so obvious when a guy likes you, then why are so many women so confused? Why is "Does He Like Me?" the most popular quiz on A New Mode? Well, one explanation was illustrated in the story above: If you want something badly enough, you can fool yourself into believing you have it, even if it's just an illusion that kinda sorta resembles the real thing.

You want a relationship with him, so you cling to any sign that he wants the same thing. You focus exclusively on tiny pieces of the puzzle instead of putting it all together to see the larger picture. When looked at individually, a puzzle piece can be completely ambiguous, so you create your own interpretation of what it means.

This obsessive line of thinking is what Eric and I often refer to as playing "emotional detective." Women will dig into their memories and observations and go through *every* detail, no matter how small and insignificant, to try to uncover a "hidden message" or "secret code" that the guy is sending. The reality is that by playing emotional detective, you usually only succeed in doing one thing: driving yourself absolutely crazy!

The problem is that it can feel like obsessing and analyzing will have some sort of payoff, like there will be a reward for all this time and energy spent attempting to figure out what's what... but there won't be. Instead, you'll feel anxious, sad, and frustrated, and it will kill your self-esteem. I mean, when has obsessing over a guy who doesn't want to be with you ever made you feel good about yourself? There's nothing empowering about it. It's crippling and defeating, not to mention, *the biggest waste of time ever!*

## About the Signs...

Maybe at this point you're thinking: "But it's not that simple! It's *so* confusing! I just want to know if he likes me... what are the signs?!"

I considered providing a list of signs that he likes you — I mean, yes, there are certain telltale signs that indicate a guy does in fact have feelings for you — but then I realized that doing so would feed into the very mindset I'm trying so hard to get you out of. It puts you back in analysis mode. It arms you with a sort of illusory yardstick with which to measure his level of interest.

Analyzing his behavior and looking for signs is *not* what creates a healthy, long-lasting relationship. When you're comparing his behavior to a checklist of signs to see if he likes you, then you can't be present and engaged. Instead, you'll be feeding into your fears and worries, and this will transmit a negative, desperate vibe.

Rather than listing the signs, I'm going to give you one whopping piece of life-changing advice: Put your focus on liking yourself and believing the types of guys you like will like you back. That is all you need to do. And when a guy doesn't like you, or doesn't ask you out after you've given him a clear opportunity to make a move, don't let that chip away at your self-esteem. All it means is he's not the right guy for you, and that's okay.

Continue to love yourself and love your life. The hottest woman to a guy is a woman who is thoroughly *happy* with who she is. If you create love from within, you will instantly and effortlessly attract love from without. Trust me on this one.

## There Are No Mixed Messages

*"If you can't figure out where you stand with someone, it might be time to stop standing and start walking."*

~ *Unknown*

What girl can forget that infamous episode of *Sex and the City* when Carrie brought her new boyfriend, Jack Berger, out to dinner with her girlfriends, and he became their Ask a Guy for a night. Even though the scene-stealing line was: "He's just not that into you," I think the line that came a little later in the conversation is even more important, when Berger says: "There are no mixed messages," after which the girls look at him in horror, eyes wide and jaws agape, their world literally turned upside down. "I've spent my life deciphering mixed messages" Miranda says, defeated. "I built a career on it!" Carrie chimes in. Well cheers to that, Carrie, because so have I. Only in mine I try to drum in the fact that there are no mixed messages. He likes you or he doesn't. He wants to be with you or he doesn't. Simple as that. Really. Truly. I promise.

At the same time, I understand the confusion. I used to *live* in that cloud of confusion. Looking at the "signs," trying to understand what they meant, reading books and articles, asking girlfriends, asking guy friends. I would read my relationships like I was reading a horoscope, latching onto the stuff that aligned with how I wanted things to be and disregarding or dismissing the rest.

In the end, the guys who liked me were the ones who clearly liked me. The guys who had my head spinning were maybe a bit interested, maybe somewhat attracted to me, but they didn't *like* me… not enough anyway.

The chords of confusion usually sound something like this: *He said one thing, but then did another… he was sweet and attentive in the beginning, but then something changed… he said he's never liked a girl so much, then he disappeared…he used to text me every day, now I hardly hear for him… we've been seeing each other for months, but I don't really know how he feels about me.* What women call "mixed messages" is actually one very clear message: He doesn't want to be with you. He may want to hang out with you, he may want to hook up with you, but that is not the same as *being with you.*

When a guy is sending confusing signals, it usually means he's either ambivalent or maybe somewhat interested… but not interested enough. And in these cases, nothing you say or do will change that. You cannot convince someone to want you, and no amount of wanting him will make him want you back. If he was iffy about you from the start, then nothing you said or did caused the relationship to end… there just wasn't enough there to begin with.

No good guy sets out to intentionally lead a woman on. I just want to clarify this point because it would be a mistake to think he's stringing you along intentionally.

Here's what usually happens in these "mixed message" scenarios. A guy meets a girl, he thinks she's attractive and cool and wants to get to know her a little more. She's fun to talk to and he enjoys hanging out with her, but he can kind of take her or leave her. He's open to exploring and seeing where things go, but he isn't gripped by an "I've gotta make her mine!" feeling. So they have some interactions, and in time he realizes he just doesn't like her enough to pursue a relationship. This is where things can start to get murky, especially if the girl is still clinging onto hope that a relationship is in the cards. Either she will waste her time analyzing his behavior and trying to figure out how he feels, or she will beat herself up, wondering what she did wrong and why she always screws things up. Or she might settle for a friends-with-benefits type of situation, or even worse, a *non-relationship* where she acts like his girlfriend even though she isn't, in the hope that he'll come around once he sees how amazing she is.

The more she invests emotionally in him, the more her sense of self-worth will become entangled in his opinion of her. If he's nice and affectionate, she's worthy. If he's cold and distant, she's worthless. She isn't her authentic self with him and instead tries to make herself into what she thinks he wants. She is careful with everything she says, worrying that something as slight as a single overeager text message might be enough to ruin everything. She clings to the hope that once she can get him to commit, she'll finally feel okay.

## Guy Confession

"Guys send out mixed messages when they like attention from a particular woman, but know deep down they won't commit to something long term. It could be because a guy knows that by keeping a girl mildly interested, but still technically within the boundaries of the "friend zone," that they've not done anything 'scumbagish.' But at the same time, the woman who thinks the guy is genuinely interested in her will get more roped in and hopeful." - Adam, 29

# "What if I Do Something to Suddenly Turn Him Off?"

A lot of women worry that doing or saying the wrong thing will send a guy from like to dislike as quick as clicking on the button on Facebook.

Here's something to keep in mind. When a guy likes you, *really* likes you, he won't be turned off by something small you say or do, and it will take a lot more than responding to his texts right away or using too many enthusiastic emojis to turn him off.

If he likes you, he won't change his mind over something small. If he's unsure of you, the small things can be enough to cause his interest to wane further. Again, nothing you can say or do will change this; if there just isn't enough fundamental chemistry and compatibility to begin with, a guy can be turned off by something small because he was never attracted enough in the first place. So there's no reason to beat yourself up, because it really isn't anything you did.

Sometimes a guy just isn't in a place where he can be in a relationship. Maybe he has deeply ingrained trust issues, maybe he just isn't ready, maybe he's struggling with his career. Or maybe he is attracted to you and interested, but just doesn't think it would work out long term because of some sort of deal-breaker (maybe you're different religions, live in different places, want different things). Everyone has their quirks, and just because one person thinks things like geography and religion are no big deal and love will conquer all, the other might feel totally differently.

I have a guy friend who is incredibly stubborn and has a firm set of values he won't compromise on. If he is dating a girl and finds that her political views are completely counter to his, he's done. He will also lose interest if a girl isn't motivated, because he strongly values a good work ethic. Not every guy is like this. There are guys who don't need partners who share their views and life values. The point I'm making is, everyone's got their something and it's *their* thing, not *your* problem.

The reasons a guy decides not to pursue a relationship don't matter. And if he isn't demonstrating he likes you in an *obvious* way, then he doesn't like you enough. Your mind might delude you into thinking that finding the answers will give you some sort of relief from your pain, but it rarely works that way. The only way to get relief is to move on with your head held high and your sense of self intact.

## Where Healthy Relationships Begin

*"True love comes quietly, without banners or flashing lights. If you hear bells, get your ears checked."*

*~ Erich Segal*

Healthy relationships don't come about through obsession or force or analysis. They just evolve effortlessly.

In the right relationship with a guy who is compatible with you, you can be yourself and behave naturally without fear of scaring him away (within reason, that is). In the wrong relationship, you feel confused and insecure, like one mistake or bad move will trip some wire and he'll leave.

If you are with a guy and feel like you have to constantly watch what you say or do, then that is a big sign he's not the right guy for you.

Relationships and love aren't hard, complicated, or filled with effort ... if what you have is like that, it's most likely because you're trying to force it to work. Movies portray love as hard and full of obstacles and drama because movies are meant for entertainment, and those scenarios are entertaining. But that's not real. Love doesn't come from struggle and drama and difficulty. In fact, true love happens and blossoms pretty effortlessly most of the time. Shakespeare's *Romeo and Juliet* was intended to be a satire on the follies of love, and instead it has endured for centuries as a tale of true love and romance!

I want to clarify that when I say it should be effortless, I'm not saying relationships don't take work. They do. But that comes later. In the beginning, if you like him and he likes you, then it just unfolds and happens naturally. You don't *make* it happen, you don't ask, and you don't wonder. You just know. You can just be. And it's the most peaceful, blissful experience.

A lasting relationship does take work, and even the best relationships won't always feel good, but occasional arguments and misunderstandings aren't the same as trying to force someone to feel a certain way, or forcing someone to make you feel a certain way. When you are compatible, you will be able to work together in the face of adversity. When you are incompatible, you will always be locked in a battle of wills, fighting against one another.

Sometimes two people simply aren't a match. You may not always understand why, but it's just the way it is. Sometimes two people are a match, but it just isn't the right time. Sometimes two people are a match and it is the right time, but they let their fears and insecurities suck the joy out of the relationship and sabotage it.

In any case, obsessing over how he feels never gets you anywhere. Stop trying to figure out how a guy feels. Any time you start spinning and looking for clues, remind yourself that if he truly liked you, you wouldn't be in this mental space. Affirm to yourself that you are loveable, and a guy not wanting to be with you does not prove otherwise.

## It's Obvious...

*"When you realize you want to spend the rest of your life with somebody, you want the rest of your life to start as soon as possible."*

~ *When Harry Met Sally*

When a man likes you and wants to be with you, he will be. He will ask you out and if it goes well and he sees potential, he will ask you out again. If he flirts with you, chats you up, tells you he thinks you're hot and cool, but doesn't ask you out, then he's probably attracted and somewhat interested, but just not enough. Don't make the mistake of thinking this means something negative about you; it doesn't. It just means he, for whatever reason, doesn't think you would be compatible... and that's fine!

Discovering you're incompatible is great. It saves you months or years of heartache and distraction and frees you up to find someone who is the right fit for you. If you're authentically being yourself — enjoying your life, doing what you love to do, being who you are — and another person shows up and loves you for who you are, you won't need to expend any effort or energy trying to impress him or trying to make yourself more acceptable to him. He will like and appreciate you for who you are, and this requires no effort on your part. The more he gets to know you, the more he will come to love you, because he will be tapping into who you are at your core, not some flimsy version of yourself that you're presenting to him.

Being liked or loved by a man can feel good, but what is it really worth if he isn't taking the steps to be with you? Maybe he has valid reasons, maybe he doesn't… it doesn't matter. Why would you even want to be with someone who doesn't want you enough to go after you full force? You want a man who wants you so badly that he isn't going to leave any sliver of empty space for some other guy to swoop in and snatch you up.

A while ago I was talking to Eric about some guy I thought liked me but wasn't asking me out. I described the details of our encounters, all of which clearly indicated he liked me, but rather than feeding me what I wanted to hear (that of course this guy liked me!), Eric said something that was so true and spot on it was burned into my brain, and I have repeated it countless times to friends and readers entangled in this type of situation. He said: "Any relationship worth being in happens because the other person can't help but want to be with you. If you don't have that, whatever you would have isn't worth it anyway." Write it down, memorize it, let it seep into your psyche, and live it. I did, and it made a huge difference in my love life.

## Make This Your Mantra

- There is one universal rule when it comes to a man's romantic interest: When a guy likes you, it's obvious.
- If you're worrying about or analyzing whether or not he likes you, you already have your answer.
- It goes against a man's nature to not pursue a woman he wants to be with, especially when he has the opportunity.
- What women call "mixed messages" are actually one very clear message: He doesn't want to be with you.
- When a guy is sending confusing signals, it usually means he's somewhat interested… but not enough.
- When you're in the wrong relationship, you're stuck in your head thinking about it. When you're in the right relationship, the impulse to worry or analyze doesn't cross your mind because you're too busy enjoying it and enjoying your life.

# Exercise

Rather than frantically trying to figure out how he feels, if he likes you, and what he meant when he said X Y or Z… consider how *you* really feel, if *you* truly like him, if he actually deserves your energy and affection. Ask yourself these questions to make sure your relationship is starting off in a healthy place:

- Do I feel better about myself and my life with this person around?
- Do I feel like he's someone I can trust?
- Do I feel like he's my partner, and on my side?
- Is it effortless to be around him (can I be totally relaxed and unguarded around him)?
- Can I be fully myself around him?
- Does he completely "get" me?

These questions are things everyone — both guys and girls — should consider before getting into a relationship. Most people know the answers on a subconscious level. When it's the right relationship, you feel at peace knowing these things are all true. When it's the wrong relationship, you feel uneasy because deep down you know the answers, but you're actively blocking them from rising to the forefront of your consciousness. This usually happens when you attach your ego and fears to a situation. You ignore the fact that this is a bad match and you can't really be yourself, and focus on how validating it will be one day to *finally* win this person's love.

The first step to having an amazing relationship is to choose wisely. If you choose someone who is incompatible with you, then no amount of relationship advice will help.

# Resources

In the resource section (www.anewmode.com/resource) for Chapter 1 you will learn *exactly* how to tell if you're with the guy who's right for you.

Articles include:

What No One Tells You About Good Relationships

What Do Guys Like in a Girl?

How to Have a Healthy Relationship

Ask a Guy: Does He Like Me?

Ask a Guy: Signs a Guy Likes You

Also! Be sure to take our shockingly accurate "Does He Like Me?" quiz (www.anewmode.com/like-me-quiz) so you know the truth once and for all.

# Chapter 2: Men Crave Appreciation

*"Love is giving people the freedom to be the way
they are, not trying to make them the way you want."*

*~ Unknown*

*How do I crack a man's code? How can I reach him deeply? I feel
like I'm putting everything into the relationship and getting nothing
back.* Does any of this sound familiar? I have certainly experienced
these frustrations. The reason it's a struggle is because men and
women often have different needs in a relationship and experience
love in different ways. A woman may get frustrated because her
guy isn't giving her what she needs, without realizing that it runs
both ways and oftentimes, she isn't giving him what he really
needs, either. We all experience the world subjectively and as a
result, we give love in the way we want to receive it... but the way
men and women experience love and what they need isn't the same.

Most women (myself included) don't fully understand how crucial
it is for a man to feel appreciated, and the enormous impact
expressions of appreciation can have on him. Granted, everyone
likes to be acknowledged and appreciated, but women don't need it
in the same way and to the same extent that men do.

Just as most women primarily need to feel cherished and adored,
men need to feel appreciated and admired to be truly satisfied in a
relationship.

## When You Know the Truth...

When you give a man what he truly needs, it allows him to be
himself and inspires him. In turn, he will naturally want to give you
more of what you need. When he feels acknowledged and
appreciated by you, he will want to acknowledge and appreciate

you in return. You will no longer be left feeling drained, like you're giving everything and getting nothing, because what you give will be received by him in a way that inspires him and makes him want to go above and beyond for you.

## Appreciation in the Early Stages of Dating

*"Before you speak, ask yourself: Is it necessary? Is it true? Does it improve upon the silence?"*

*~ Shirdi Sai Baba*

Women and men have very different thought processes in the early courtship phase. Women typically measure a man against some sort of mental checklist… if he checks enough of her boxes then she gets excited about the possibility of being in a relationship. Men don't really measure women this way. Granted, every guy has certain preferences when it comes to physical characteristics and personality traits, but what a man considers more than anything else is how he feels around a woman. It's about how she connects to who he truly is, to his core essence. When he feels like she is genuinely interested in *him*, not in what he represents or in his potential as a boyfriend, then he becomes more interested, unguarded, and invested.

A lot of us get so concerned with seeming interesting to the guy that we don't show enough genuine interest in and appreciation for *him*. Our egos can be fragile. We want to protect ourselves and we want him to like us, so we put on a bit of a show and go into dates thinking of ways to dazzle him. This is fine to an extent — all people present themselves in the best light during the early courtship phases — but it's also important to show interest in him and discover what he's all about. It is only when you do this that his guard will come down a bit and he will feel safe enough to connect with you in a meaningful way.

I have a close friend I'll call Nick. He isn't a heartbreaker, per se; he's just so lovable that girls can't help but fall for him and are left devastated if he doesn't reciprocate. It's not intentional on his part, he is just very good at creating surface chemistry, and a lot of girls get caught up in it and take it to mean they share a special connection, even though this is something he can create with just about anyone. The trouble he has with relationships is that girls get so seduced by his external charm they can't, or don't try, to see beyond it. Nick has dated many amazing girls, but there's only been one who truly captured his heart, one girl he ever seriously thought he could marry. I asked him what it was about her that inspired these feelings and he said:

"She was just such an appreciator. She would listen to my music and quote my own song lyrics back to me, and I was just like, 'Whoa! You're a goddess.' She would ask me what each line meant, and she truly wanted to know what inspired each song, each note, each word. She was just such a fan and 'got' me on multiple levels. Some of it was instant and a product of our having a strong connection, but a lot of it was the result of her really trying to understand me, and that's what made her stand out from the rest."

Showing genuine interest in a guy is about tapping into his likes, his interests, his passions, his goals. It's about finding out what drives him and why. Try to really get to know him. Get to know the man underneath the mask and appreciate him for who he is — not what he has, not his surface-level accomplishments, not his success or popularity — who he is at his core. Discover his values, his motivations, what he wants out of life and how he goes about achieving it, and appreciate him for these things.

Try to listen more than you speak. This isn't always easy for us as we are usually the more verbal gender, but it's important to step back sometimes and let him fill in the empty space. When he speaks, give him your full attention and try to focus on what he's saying instead of thinking about what you want to say next.

Be open to his world and recognize what's meaningful to him. Figure out what he wants in his life and what his goals are, and support his efforts to achieve them. When you become his confidante, he will share his feelings and what he's going through. Some days will be good, others won't. What every man wants is a woman who will be there through the good and the bad, a woman he can share ideas with, a woman who will support him no matter what.

## Guy Confession

"I met a girl on Tinder and asked her on a date after some back-and-forth messaging and a wonderful phone conversation. We went on an awesome first date and shared a wonderful kiss at the end. She talked very fast and quite a bit, but I didn't hold it against her because she told me she was feeling nervous. I took her to a nice restaurant for our second date... she was still talking quite a bit and this time I was starting to notice. I tried to manufacture interest in the conversation, which was becoming increasingly difficult since I didn't really get a turn to talk. We went to a friend's party after dinner, and holding a conversation was becoming even more difficult. Where is the girl I talked to on the phone? I can't seem to find any interests in common, and she doesn't even ask me questions or seem remotely curious about the things I think about. I offer up some stories here and there, talk about stuff I'm passionate about… she nods and smiles and waits for her turn to talk.

By midnight I'm totally exhausted and feel uncomfortable in her presence. I try not to be rude and continue to put on a good face so it doesn't get weird.

She was a nine when I met her, now she's a six at most… I'm noticing physical details I don't like, and I realize this is because my attraction to her personality is slipping… aaand it's gone. I was extremely into this girl but the magic of our first date went up in smoke by the second one." - Brian, 32

## Appreciation in a Relationship

Women who don't know how essential appreciation is to a man can cause irreparable harm to their relationship. Maybe she expects him to do certain things and gets angry when he doesn't, or demands he do certain things and then nags him for not doing it right. She believes she's putting effort into the relationship (usually what we consider "effort" is really a lot of pointless analyzing and obsessing and trying to figure him out… which serves no positive purpose) while he isn't pulling his weight. He feels defeated and unappreciated, so he retreats and does even less. The last thing she wants to do when he is failing to meet her needs is show him any sort of appreciation, because why should she?! Instead she'll berate him about all the things he isn't doing right, hoping it will force him to get off his bum and take some action. But it has the opposite effect — he becomes even less motivated. She resents him for not doing what she wants, and he resents her for nagging him and making him feel like a pathetic loser. This cycle can continue indefinitely until one or both parties gains a deeper understanding of what the other truly needs.

When you express appreciation to a man for the things he does, he will do even more. That's because appreciation taps into the deepest core of a man. It's not just about saying "thank you" when he does something nice, although that's important. Really appreciating a man comes down to seeing who he truly is at his core, not just on the surface. It is about seeing what he has to offer, not just superficially, but emotionally, intellectually, physically, and spiritually, and genuinely appreciating it.

## Seeing Behind the Mask

We all wear masks in the world; they protect us from being vulnerable, from getting hurt, from being rejected. The "masks" we wear are similar to social media sites in that they let us project an image of who we want to be... and this isn't always in alignment with who we truly are. The got-it-together smooth-talking, charismatic, successful guy might be painfully insecure deep down. Everyone has a story that is so much richer and more complex than what you see from the outside looking in.

The reality is that he's the man underneath "the mask," the man who feels strong emotions about the things that actually matter to him. He is a man who wants to be seen and understood and appreciated for who he really is.

Most men feel lonely and misunderstood on some level. It's not that they don't feel comfortable talking about their emotions, it's that much of the time they don't even know how to access those emotions. But feelings don't disappear just because they go unacknowledged. So he goes through life with a feeling that something's not quite right, and he thinks no woman will ever accept him for who he is, that he will always have to maintain a façade to keep up appearances. He's afraid if he reveals himself, a woman won't like what she sees, and he'll be abandoned and alone. When he finds a woman who gets him, who understands and appreciates him, who sees his depth and rather than being turned off feels even more attracted to him... something shifts and he experiences an inner peace that has always evaded him. He feels like everything is okay, like he's worthy, and he breathes a huge sigh of relief.

When a woman sees and acknowledges a man for all those things that everyone else ignores, it has a profound effect on him. It's not about appreciating a man for his material wealth or surface-level accomplishments or any of those superficial things that are all subject to change. Your being impressed that he has a high-powered job will feel good, but can also create an underlying fear within him that if he loses the job you will be disappointed and won't think as highly of him. If instead you are impressed by his work ethic, his motivation, or his ability to accomplish anything he sets his mind to, for instance, then there is no fear, because you are appreciating his inherent qualities, qualities that will still be there even if his life circumstances change. Truly appreciating a man is about appreciating and acknowledging the "goodness" in him in a way that inspires him to be his best self.

No matter what your relationship status is, try to find specific things to appreciate about your guy. Saying he is kind, considerate, smart, loyal, etc. doesn't have a huge impact on a man because in his mind, there are plenty of guys out there who can be described in the same way. Look for specific things he does, or specific things about him, that make *him* special, that make *him* irreplaceable in your eyes, and acknowledge those things.

# Appreciating What He Does

*"We cannot change anything unless we accept it.*
*Condemnation does not liberate, it oppresses."*

*~ Carl Jung*

No man, no matter how amazing, caring, romantic, and compatible, is going to get it right every single time. He is never going to be able to do exactly what you want in the exact way you want him to do it because A) he's not a mind reader and B) he has been shaped by a whole different set of experiences that cause him to give and receive love in different ways than you. Many times a guy will do something with the intention of making you happy, and will be shocked to find it had the opposite effect.

A friend of mine recently had an experience that illustrates this point. She called me up furious after her boyfriend gave her a beautiful necklace. Why the fury? Well, her boyfriend has this drawer filled with treasures he has accumulated over the years. One night he reached into the drawer and gave her a necklace he got years ago. She didn't even pause before reacting, and her initial reaction was to be hurt. "He should have gone out and bought a necklace specifically for me that he knew *I* would like. It just seems like laziness to give me something he bought before he even met me!" she explained. It took me some time before I could fully understand why she was so upset, because I saw his gesture as incredibly romantic. He had given her something that was special and significant to him, something he'd had for many years that no other woman was worthy of receiving. But my friend just couldn't see it that way. She appreciated the gesture to an extent, but she really would have preferred for him to buy something especially for her.

The story reminded me of a similar experience I had many years ago when I was in my first very serious relationship. One night my boyfriend reached into a drawer and pulled out a beautiful ring that had come into his possession many years earlier and told me, "When I got this ring, I never thought I'd find someone special enough to give it to, until you." I was beaming; it was the most romantic thing a guy had ever done for me.

The point is, we all have different desires and expectations in relationships. And if we expect our partner to get it right every single time, and punish him whenever he gets it wrong, then we will end up in an unhappy, resentment-filled relationship.

You may not even realize all the ways your expectations are preventing you from enjoying the relationship and feeling his love. Rather than looking at his intent we often look at his action, and if the action isn't what we think he *should* have done, then we get upset. This makes the guy feel like nothing he does naturally, from the heart, will ever be enough; he feels defeated and eventually stops trying.

When you appreciate him for his efforts — even small ones like taking out the trash — he feels inspired and on top of the world. He feels significant and wants more of that feeling, so he tries harder to make you happy.

A lot of us can't help but reflexively react, and this causes so many unnecessary fights. A much smarter strategy is to take a step back and try to see the intentions behind his actions. Most of the time, he intended to make you happy. Maybe he didn't text you back right away this one time, but think about all the other times he texted you just to say hi and see how your day was going. Maybe he didn't buy you a dozen roses on your anniversary, but he took you to that restaurant you said you've been dying to try. Maybe he didn't show up at your door with chicken soup and tissues when you had a bad cold, but he called and texted throughout the day to check up on you and see how you were feeling. When you can train yourself to look at what he *is* doing right — instead of zeroing in on other ways he could have gone above and beyond — you will find much more peace and happiness in your relationship, and your man will feel appreciated and significant and will come to love you even more.

When he does something you like, appreciate it... don't expect it or act entitled. Acting entitled can be as much of a motivation killer for a man as nagging. All you need to do is show genuine appreciation in a way that reaches him deeply. You don't need to do something for him when he does something for you. Relationships aren't based on quid pro quo. Just expressing your genuine gratitude and appreciation is all he needs.

No matter how far into a relationship you are, never stop showing appreciation. Even if you have been together for years and he picks up the check every single time, always be sure to thank him for it and tell him you appreciate it.

## Guy Confession

"I started dating a girl I saw a lot of potential with. She was my type physically and had a fun, upbeat, positive attitude that was great to be around. In the beginning, I was a bit bothered by the fact that she never really said thank you for anything. I mean, I enjoyed taking her out on nice dates, but it would have been nice to hear a genuine thank you at the end. As time went on, I couldn't see past it anymore and my feelings started to change. She never showed appreciation for *anything!* One night she suggested we stay in and make dinner at her apartment, and she also asked if her roommate could join. Even though it was her idea, she had me go out and buy all the groceries and do all the cooking, and she didn't show an ounce of appreciation. I was done after that, and officially ended it about a week later." - Zack, 33

# Men Need Respect

*"The greatest happiness of life is the conviction that
we are loved; loved for ourselves, or rather, loved in
spite of ourselves."*

*~ Victor Hugo*

No, I don't mean he needs you to obey him and cater to his every whim. Respect can really be understood as another incarnation of appreciation. Respect is a two-way street, of course; women need respect too, but for different things. Men need to be respected for being competent and able to achieve goals and figure things out. This is why men typically get annoyed if women try to tell them what to do or how to live their lives; the old stereotype of men not asking for directions exists for a reason!

A man also needs to feel like his girl has his best interests at heart — that she can give him space when he needs it, doesn't always prioritize her needs over his, and respects his wishes.

What makes a man feel loved is when a woman can show him this respect and appreciation, both when he's doing what she wants and when he isn't. This doesn't mean you should condone bad behavior. It means you still see the goodness within him, even when his behavior isn't good. There is a big difference between disapproving of an action and disapproving of him *as a person*.

When a woman respects a man, she understands who he is and what he needs and gives him space to express himself, without constantly making demands on him and prioritizing her needs over his.

Respect means accepting that he needs certain things, even if they are in opposition to what *you* want or need. For example, when men get stressed out or feel unbalanced, they usually like to retreat into their "cave" to sort things out. They don't necessarily like talking through the problem, and would instead rather work it out on their own and then come back into the relationship recharged.

So let's say your guy is having a hard time and needs some time alone, but you really want him to be open and honest with you and to share his feelings. Respecting him entails putting what's best for him above what you want. In this case, it would be giving him the space he needs to work through his issues, even though you would prefer that he talk to you about it. This is who he is and what's going to be most beneficial for him. Asking him to handle stress in a way that's contrary to his nature isn't respecting who he is — it's asking him to be something he's not. Doing this to a man will not draw him to you and make you closer, it will push him away.

When you appreciate your man and are able to see him for who he is and love him for being that person, flaws and all, even when it conflicts with what you want, you are empowering him and empowering yourself, too. When a woman is in a good place emotionally, she can do this effortlessly because it comes naturally to her. She brings out the best in him because she is coming from a place of love, not a place of control. She doesn't need him to validate her sense of self or be the one to heal her from her painful past. She is with him because she *wants* to be, not because she has an agenda. If his natural way of being conflicts often and painfully with what she wants, the answer isn't to try to force him to be something he's not, it's to decide if there is an issue of compatibility.

## Why Is It So Hard to Appreciate?

Showing appreciation is easy in theory but hard in practice. Sometimes we're just too annoyed and frustrated by our man to summon even a stitch of appreciation for anything, and a part of us may even feel like he doesn't deserve it.

An important thing to realize is that often when we feel upset or disappointed by a guy, it's actually a reflection of how we feel about ourselves. We don't feel good about ourselves and we want him to give us assurances that we are worthy and lovable, to prop up our sense of self-worth. When he doesn't, we blame him for "making" us feel a certain way.

We tell ourselves things like, *If he really cared about me, he would be doing X, Y and Z; if he doesn't do those things, then that means he doesn't care.* When you create these sorts of expectations, you set your man up to fail. If you don't trust that he really cares about you, nothing he does will ever convince you otherwise.

The reason most of us have such a hard time pushing past a man's walls and reaching him deeply is that we fixate on our own wants, our own worries, our own fears, our own needs, and pay no attention to how he feels and experiences things. This causes us to essentially see a guy as an object rather than an autonomous human being. When we objectify someone in this way, we only see him in terms of how he can serve us for a specific purpose, and this is the opposite of respect. When this happens, we are no longer seeing him as the unique person he is in the world, with his own needs, goals, and dreams; instead, we're seeing him only in terms of the role he plays for us, how his actions affect us, what he can do for us.

Maybe you want him to act a certain way so you will feel worthwhile, maybe you want to feel desired, maybe you want to feel worthy of love… and you become resentful when he doesn't do the things that will make you feel this way. You feel like you're giving everything to the relationship and getting nothing back. You can't appreciate him for what he does, because what he does isn't exactly the thing that will make you feel the way you want to feel. What he is doing is never enough — all you see is what he *isn't* doing.

When you genuinely appreciate someone, it means you appreciate his essence, and this isn't contingent on him doing exactly what you want in order to make you feel a certain way.

The mind can be a tricky and menacing thing. When it starts spinning and churning out negative thoughts, painful emotions ensue. You feel sad, hurt, and angry, and you may interpret these feelings as facts and proof that your guy did something wrong. But so often these feelings are self-generated and based in our own fears and insecurities; it might not be what he did that made you upset, but the meaning you attached to his behavior.

If you find yourself reflexively getting upset over small things (he took too long to text back... he wanted a night out with the boys... he didn't call to say goodnight... he didn't compliment you on your appearance when you got all glammed up one night), it's a sign that you feel unloved or insecure in the relationship, but that doesn't mean it's his fault, or that it's his job to behave differently to make you feel loved and secure. If you are in a committed relationship and you know he loves you and is invested in the relationship, and you still feel this way over small things, it means these feelings are coming from some unresolved issues in your past, or pain and insecurity within you. The responsibility to deal with this and fix it also lies within you — not within him.

If you're in an uncommitted relationship, you may feel even less secure, and instead of being present in the relationship, which would allow it to turn into whatever it's meant to become, you may unknowingly be in "agenda mode."

For example, if you're dating a guy and he isn't ready to call you his girlfriend, you may view being "official" as a goal and treat it as such. When this mindset takes hold, you stop appreciating him for who he is, and instead measure his actions in terms of whether they are getting you closer to, or further from, your goal. If he does something nice, you appreciate him, but only because he's giving you a sign that you are moving toward your goal. If he isn't giving you indications that your relationship is heading toward being "official," in line with your goal, you punish him (either by putting up a wall and giving him an "I'm fine" when he asks what's wrong, or by being confrontational and attacking him). This effectively sabotages the relationship because he feels unappreciated, and he knows on some level that you only view him as a means to an end. The same dynamic can also come into play when you're in a long-term relationship and your guy isn't taking the next step when you think it's time.

I want to add that I am not pointing fingers and placing blame. For a relationship to be truly healthy, happy, and long lasting, both men and women need to work on becoming their best selves. It's about recognizing our pain and insecurities and trying to work through them, rather than letting them become the lens through which we view our relationships and expecting the other person to cater to them. I'm not placing the responsibility for this all on women; much of what I'm saying applies to both genders equally, but I am focusing on women because, well… this book is written for women.

I had to learn these lessons the hard way. I couldn't understand why I was always so chronically dissatisfied in my relationships… even in relationships with really great guys who adored me. No matter what, I always found something wrong, some reason to be unhappy. The truth is, I was struggling with my own self-esteem issues, and deep down I didn't feel truly worthy of love. When you don't feel like you deserve love, you won't be able to let it in, period.

## Make This Your Mantra

- Appreciation opens up the guy and makes him want to make you feel as good as you make him feel. It creates a relationship dynamic that gets deeper and more inspiring... (and the opposite vibe creates the opposite result).

- Appreciating a man comes down to seeing who he truly is and appreciating him at his core. It means acknowledging the person who exists beneath the surface mask he wears out in the world.

- The more he feels that you appreciate him, the more he will want to do for you. Tell him when he does something that makes you feel good, or be direct and tell him exactly what you want.

- Most men feel lonely and misunderstood on some level. When you take the time to appreciate him for who he is, you become irreplaceable.

- When you genuinely appreciate a guy, it means you appreciate his essence, and this isn't contingent on him doing exactly what you want or making you feel a certain way.

## Exercise

1. Try showing genuine appreciation for who your man is and the things he does. Look for specific things that are unique to him. When expressing appreciation for the things he does for you, be specific and tell him how it makes you feel: "I love it when you do X, it really makes me feel Y."

2. When you feel upset or angry by something your guy did, pause before reacting and try to get to the root of why you're upset. Try the following:

- Observe and notice your thoughts, instead of letting them spin out of control.

- Distinguish feelings from facts.

- Any time he says or does something that hurts you, write it down and contemplate it, instead of immediately saying something to him about it. Do this for a few weeks and see if you notice any recurring patterns.

This will give you insight into your inner world, and you will be able to better identify where your hurt is really coming from. By doing this, you may discover that most of the recurring fights and disagreements that occur in your relationship are the result of one or several underlying causes within you that have gone unaddressed.

## Resources

Check out the resource page (www.anewmode.com/resource) for Chapter 2 to learn more about what men really want and need in a relationship, how to get better at showing appreciation, and how to get the love you want.

Articles include:

5 Ways to Ruin a Budding Relationship

Ask a Guy: Why Is He With Me?

How Gratitude Can Save Your Relationship

Ask a Guy: How Do I Find Love?

# Chapter 3: Men Need to Feel Like Winners

*"If you treat an individual as he is, he will stay as he is, but if you treat him as if he were what he ought to be and could be, he will become what he ought to be and could be."*

*~ Goethe*

When I tell people what I do for a living, they always ask for the most surprising or important thing I've learned about men through writing about relationships. This chapter is the long version of my answer: Men need to feel like winners.

I honestly never knew or even considered how vital it is for a man to feel like a winner. I never saw it discussed or even hinted at in magazines or relationship books, and it certainly isn't something men tell you outright. Until you know it, it gets completely overlooked. Once you know it, however, you will see it in everything he does.

Women who don't know this about men can't understand why he sometimes doesn't seem as invested in the relationship as they are. They may feel dismissed when he makes other things in his life a higher priority. They don't understand why he sometimes shuts down and withdraws, why he won't talk about things when he's having a hard time. They take this to mean he doesn't care and doesn't feel close to them, and this is hurtful to women.

When a woman feels hurt, she may lash out or punish her guy by withholding love or going cold on him. She doesn't realize that this only adds to his stress and makes him feel like more of a loser.

# When You Know the Truth...

You won't feel like he isn't prioritizing you or doesn't care... you'll realize that relationships, while very important, usually come second in the world of men. Being a winner comes first. This doesn't mean he doesn't love you and adore you and worship you. It means that feeling like a winner is essential to his sense of self and sense of self-worth. If he doesn't have that, he will never be able to be the man you need, the one who can make you happy. Instead, he will be caught in a web of defeat and misery.

Sometimes he will need to prioritize feeling like a winner over being emotionally available to you. A woman who doesn't know this will get on his case and accuse him of not caring and not putting any effort into the relationship. What you need to realize (and will throughout this chapter) is that him feeling like a winner *is* him putting effort into the relationship. He needs to feel like a winner in the world in order to be the best partner he can for you.

## Personal Story

I fell in love for the first time when I was 20 (the relationship I referenced in the introduction). He was smart, insightful, sensitive, beautiful, and, unfortunately, a total mess. We met a week after he had been dumped by a girl he really loved, and on top of that he was failing miserably at a job he hated. Being young and naive and having no real understanding of what love is except for what I'd seen in the movies, I thought my love could heal him somehow. I thought if I loved him enough, he would snap out of his funk and be the man I knew he could be.

But I went about loving him all wrong. Instead of encouraging him to get his act together, I tried to take care of everything for him. I thought if I made his life as easy and manageable as possible, he would love me even more and suddenly find the motivation to get his life in order. I paid for our dates because he couldn't afford to, I did his laundry because he couldn't afford to, I cleaned his apartment, I fixed his resume, I searched for job listings online and applied to them for him. I kept doing and doing for him and was baffled about why he remained stuck in his rut. Even after all this, and even though we spent pretty much all our time together, he wouldn't call me his girlfriend… but I stayed, and I continued to be the best "girlfriend" in the whole world, hoping that one day I would be worthy of the title. I held onto the hope that as soon as he got a job… as soon as he snapped out of his depression… as soon as he started taking better care of himself… then finally we would have a fairy-tale romance.

After many months of things going from bad to worse, of our once passion-filled relationship drying up and turning into an almost platonic, mother-son type of dynamic, he cheated on me and swiftly entered into a relationship with the other woman. If that wasn't bad enough, within a few weeks of dating her he suddenly transformed into the man he never was with me! He got a real job, he committed to her (even on Facebook, which he'd always told me he would never, ever do with any girl), he took her on romantic dates. He was happy and alive. I felt devastated and beat myself up over it for months. What did she have that I didn't have? Where did I go wrong? Why wasn't I good enough?

The answers didn't come until several years later, with both the wisdom that comes from experience and my somewhat hasty decision to reach out to him and ask the questions that had been haunting me. The short version of this very long conversation is that while he did care for me and even love me, being with me made him feel like an even bigger loser. The more I tried to "fix" him, the more damaged he felt. The more I did for him, the more useless he felt. The more I tried to make his life easier, the more comfortable he became with his own misery.

So why her? Well, she didn't do any of those things. She saw the goodness in him and appreciated it, and through that was able to empower him without really saying or doing anything. He knew that in order to keep her he would have to step up and get it together. He knew she wouldn't tolerate a man acting like a child — waking up past noon every day and spending days on end playing video games instead of finding a job or doing something meaningful with his time. I accepted him at his worst, and so his worst self is what I got. She quietly expected him to be better (again, not with words, just in vibes) and so he felt motivated and inspired to be his best.

As sweet and accepting and loving as I was, he felt like a loser when he was around me. She expected greatness from him, and this made him believe he was great.

At the time, I thought the relationship ended because I wasn't good enough. Once I learned how vital it is for a man to feel like a winner, I was able to look back and see how I made him feel like a huge loser. It was never my intention, my intentions were always pure and good… I just didn't know any better.

## Every Man Has a Mission

*"Because the man's priority is his mission, he will always gravitate to a woman whom he feels will most support his mission."*

~ *David Deida*

Every man has a mission. The missions vary, but the fact that every man has one is true across the board. Not every man is actively pursuing his mission; instead he might be filling his days with endless distractions. But when he does something to pursue his mission, he feels alive and he feels like a winner. He feels connected to his essence. He feels like his life has purpose and meaning. His mission is related to his life's purpose; it's something that challenges him and makes him feel like he's having an impact on the world.

Men need to feel like they are conquering, like they are achieving their mission, like their efforts are paying off. When a man feels that his contribution to the world is useless, he will be in a state of despair. Relationships are very important to men, but feeling like a winner is *essential*.

Men in general are attracted on a mental, emotional, and psychological level to women who are interested in them... specifically, interested in their *mission* in life. What is it that's meaningful to him? What does he want to achieve? What does he want out of life? When you are interested in that part of his life, it energizes him. It makes him want to share himself with you and makes him feel like you're in his corner. It makes him believe he can be the man he's always aspired to be, that he can be a winner.

When a guy feels that you are intensely interested in his feelings about things he enjoys, he'll want to share with you. The more intensely interested you are, the more he'll want to share with you... and the more he shares, the more he'll bond with you.

## What It Means to Be a Winner in the World

Most of us don't understand that men move through life with a different set of goggles on. While we women tend to focus on our experiences and what they mean to us, a man's primary focus is if a certain experience gets him closer to a goal or sets him back. He doesn't dwell on what the experience *means* to him, only on what it will *do* for him.

A man's inner monologue is often: *Am I winning or losing?* For women, the question is usually: *Do I feel loved or unloved?* Winning is to men what feeling loved is to women. Women measure worth in terms of personal relationships, men measure worth in terms of their ability to have an impact on the world.

Countless studies have shown that men primarily gain their sense of worth from their ability to have an impact on the world. If a man feels like his contributions are meaningless, he will feel hopeless and may become depressed. It has been shown that women typically gain their self-esteem through their interpersonal relationships. If a woman feels that no one cares for her, or that she has no meaningful connections in her life, she will often experience despair and sadness. It makes sense, when you think about it. Women are typically much better at building connections; we're wired this way. Men are wired to go out and conquer. This is a key difference between men and women that manifests itself in countless ways in relationships.

Guys will work themselves to the bone, give themselves heart attacks, and sacrifice everything so that they don't lose. Some men will risk everything they've got in order to win at all costs. Look at how many sports heroes have been busted taking steroids or other performance-enhancing drugs. These men risked everything — their careers, their health, their reputations — just to win. To a guy, losing is crippling: It feels like his world is collapsing, like his heart is shattering and his spirit is being broken.

The relentless need to win and to avoid losing at all cost drives men in a way that most women can't fully understand. Women don't want to lose or be unsuccessful, but imagine if winning made you feel like you were on top of the world, and losing made you feel like your whole world was falling apart. How would you live your life? That's the world of winning and losing, the world that men live in.

When a man feels like a winner in the world, he feels in control of his life. He feels strong, confident and worthy of love. When a man feels like a loser in the world, he feels weak and insecure and wants to isolate himself. When he feels significant, he feels successful, and when he feels successful he feels inspired and motivated to be his best.

The drive to win and conquer is hardwired into a man and is also strongly enforced by society. Most men will admit that they feel enormous pressure to succeed. The parallel would be the pressure on women to be thin and beautiful. Everywhere we look, the message we receive is that being beautiful makes us worthy. Men get that same message about success and power. Look at some of the most popular TV shows. You have characters like Don Draper, Gregory House, Walter White, Hank Moody, Frank Underwood… none exactly what you would describe as nice people, but they can act however they want and get away with it because they offer something of immense value, and this gives them power.

A lot of people misinterpret being a winner has having a successful career. This isn't exactly what it's about, though; it's about having a feeling of achievement. The best feeling in the world for a man is to feel like he is significant and working to achieve a goal. He doesn't need to be making tons of money or climbing the corporate ladder to feel this way. And if a man doesn't feel like he's achieving a goal, or if he feels like his efforts are meaningless, he will be utterly miserable, and not even a relationship with the most amazing woman on the face of the planet will change that.

# A Man Wants a Woman Who Makes Him Feel Like a Winner

*"There comes that mysterious meeting in life when someone acknowledges who we are and what we can be, igniting the circuits of our highest potential."*

*~ Rusty Berkus*

Let's take a tour of man world. You wake up early, go to work, maybe you hate your job or maybe you love it. Either way, it's a big part of your life; it's where you spend the majority of your time. You go to meetings, you work on projects, you deal with being criticized, with your ideas being shut down, with your boss making backhanded comments. All of these things gradually chip away at you, but you summon your reserve strength and motivation and keep plugging away.

Some days you win, and those are the good days. Some days you lose, and those are the miserable days, the ones that make you want to just give up. Most days you neither win nor lose, you just exist. You go through the motions, you exert all your effort and your energy, but a tangible payoff rarely comes. At the end of the day, you're exhausted physically and emotionally. You come home and your significant other unleashes a litany of demands. She wants to know why you're home so late, why you forgot to pick up the dry cleaning *again*, why you haven't taken her out on a date in a while, why you didn't text her back when she texted you, why you didn't do this, why you did that. You just want to dig a hole and bury yourself in it. You feel like a worthless loser. You just can't get anything right.

Or, you come home and your significant other asks with a smile, "How was your day, sweetheart?" You tell her it was okay, you don't really want to get into it. She doesn't press you, she just gives you a hug and a kiss and says, "Well you are amazing at what you do, no one else can do that job better. Oh and thank you so much for (insert something nice he did), it really meant a lot to me." You go into a private room or office to unwind on your own and she leaves you be, respecting your personal space. Slowly, you start to feel calm, at ease, like everything is going to be okay. Yeah, maybe work is tough, but you have an amazing woman who is in your corner, who sees your potential, who believes in you and sees you as the man you want to be, and you feel lucky and grateful. You want to show her how much you care about her so you exit the man cave and say, "How about going somewhere really nice tonight for dinner?"

I know some of you might misinterpret this and think I'm saying you should bend over backwards to make your man happy while suppressing all your own needs. That is *not* the message I'm trying to convey. What I'm trying to illustrate is the enormous impact having a woman in his corner can have on a man, and how if you care about meeting his needs, he will care about meeting yours.

There will be times when he annoys you or frustrates you, and that's fine. And you can absolutely voice your concerns, but it has to be coming from the right place and done in the right way. It's not what you say, it's the *way* you say it that causes 95% of conflicts in relationships (this isn't just for women, the same goes for men. It's a general principle about communication). For instance, saying (in a nice, gentle tone), "I know you've been really stressed out and busy at work, but I would really appreciate it if you would pick up the dry cleaning on your way home, it would help me out a lot" is *much* more effective than saying "Why didn't you pick up the dry cleaning? I asked you to do one small thing! Fine, I'll just do it myself!"

The first scenario acknowledges his current circumstances and compassionately asks something of him while letting him know he

47

will be appreciated for completing said task (appreciation is the number one motivator for men every time). The second comes from a demanding, accusatory place, and the subtext is that he is useless and can't do anything right. His reflexive response will naturally be: "Why bother?"

Contrary to what TV portrays, most men *are* looking to find one great girl to be with. But to a man, a relationship means being with a woman who makes him feel like a winner. It means being with a woman whose presence makes him feel stronger, more confident, and more capable than when he is on his own.

When it comes to what a man wants from a relationship, he ultimately wants a woman in his corner who believes in him and who *always* sees him as the winner he wants to be in the world. Even when he feels like a loser. Even when he's going through tough times. Even when there's been a major setback and his world is falling apart. Every man on Earth has dreams he wishes he were pursuing. Few men do, though, because they fall into a passive comfort zone, maybe thinking, "What's the point?" Then they fill their lives with meaningless pursuits because they don't realize that pursuing their deepest aspiration is what would give them true fulfillment.

When a woman sees his potential and ambitions and believes in him and inspires him to pursue those things because he matters and he is a great man who is capable of doing great things… then the relationship dynamic changes tremendously in the woman's favor.

If you want a great relationship with a man, you need to always remember that for him, his experience of life centers on winning. When he's winning, he feels untouchable. But when he's losing, his world is a dark, unforgiving place. Let him know you believe in him and his power to achieve his aspirations.

# When He Feels Like a Loser...

When a man feels like he's disappointing you or failing you, it's crippling. You'll notice him withdraw and shut down, and you may have no idea why.

At least that was the case for me before I knew how crucial it is for men to feel like winners.

Guys are highly sensitive to the way you respond and react to them. If he says something and you cringe or roll your eyes, or shoot him down or give him a look that says: "That was the most moronic thing I've ever heard," it crushes him. Some men are much more sensitive to these things than others. The more insecure the guy, the more sensitive he'll be. But the fact remains that most men want to impress and dazzle you. They want to be your hero, your white knight. They want to feel like they're enriching your life in a significant way.

He wants to feel like he's enhancing your life in all areas — physically, sexually, emotionally, intellectually, spiritually and so forth. While we ladies typically respond best to compliments about who we are, men are most receptive to compliments about what they do and what they can provide (which in turn translates to how he enhanced your life). For instance, you may not even realize how thrilling it is to a man when you say, "That restaurant was delicious, that was a great choice!" This is the kind of thing that makes a man feel like he can win at making you happy, at giving you amazing experiences, at showing you new things. He wants to feel like he's the greatest thing that ever happened to you (and vice versa, of course).

Conversely, if he takes you out and you complain about the food or say the service was slow, it crushes him. It seems illogical; I mean, it's not like he *owns* the restaurant or *cooked* the food. But it was still *his* choice of restaurant and maybe it sounds silly to us, but men gain a lot of satisfaction from making the right choices, the ones that will make us happy.

It is often instinctual to love others the way we like to be loved. Most women feel loved when a man is caring and affectionate and does nice and romantic things for them. Guys aren't really like this. That's not to say they don't enjoy those things, but affection and romance don't tap into the most vital need of a man. The most essential need for a man is to feel significant and needed. Now don't misunderstand what I'm saying — making a man feel needed does not equate to acting *needy*. Needing a man means you recognize that he is someone of tremendous value who can enhance your life in significant ways. Being needy means you don't trust that he will be able to meet your needs and you place demands and expectations on him that he can't possibly fulfill. These demands are often rooted in your own fears and insecurities and come from your needing him to fill a void within you, one that only you can fill, and then getting angry with him for not doing it right. Being with a woman who is needy and desperate is draining to a man. Being with a woman who sees what he has to offer and appreciates him for it inspires him and makes him feel like the ultimate winner.

Saying, "I love you" to a man feels nice, but it doesn't have anywhere near the same impact as saying, "I admire the man you are." Men generally feel loved through appreciation and admiration. If you really want to reach him and connect to his heart, those are the areas you need to hit.

It took me a long time to recognize what really reaches a man. I was single for many years and developed an "I don't need anyone" mentality. I know I'm resourceful and I know I can make it on my own and thrive. At the same time, I realize a relationship is a partnership, and the benefit of having a partner is you don't have to do everything on your own.

50

Learning how to make your man feel like a winner can take a little time since everyone is different, but here are four easy and guaranteed ways to generate that feeling in him (as with all my advice, this should not be used as a ploy to make him fall for you. It has to come from a sincere, genuine place):

**Trust his judgment**. Even if you don't agree, try to see his point of view and at least validate where he's coming from.

**Ask for his advice**. Nothing lights a man up like feeling useful and effective. Asking for his advice or input lets him know you value his opinions and insights.

**Show appreciation for everything he does**. Don't take it for granted or expect it; show him that his efforts aren't going unnoticed and you do see and acknowledge them. Appreciate him for what he does for you, for how he lives his life, for the things he strives to achieve. Try to see everything through a filter of gratitude and appreciation. For one, you will be much happier in your relationship and overall. For another, it will alleviate his longstanding fear of not being good enough.

**Don't undermine or belittle him...** *especially* not in front of other people! If you undermine him, it will cause him to completely shut down because he will feel like a child being scolded by mommy for being a bad boy... not exactly the kind of feeling that fills a man with burning desire.

## The Main Reason Men Cheat

Men usually don't cheat because they're scumbags or scoundrels. It's not because they can't control themselves and oftentimes is not even because they no longer desire you. Men are usually tempted to cheat when they no longer feel like winners in their relationship.

He may feel like you no longer desire him sexually, like you're not turned on by him, like you don't appreciate him, like you're disappointed in him, like you aren't impressed by him. If these feelings converge with him meeting a woman who *is* turned on by him, who does value him, who does appreciate him, who makes him feel like a *man,* well…

Cheating is usually the result of an easy opportunity and him feeling like a loser, either in life or in his relationship. In order to feel valuable and significant again, he may give in to temptation, even if he really loves his partner. This is a testament to how vital a man's need to feel like a winner is. Men will often sacrifice things that they hold truly dear, simply to temporarily stop feeling like a loser.

Women typically cheat when they no longer feel seen, loved, or cared for. A woman whose emotional needs are being fully met is very unlikely to cheat. For a man… it really comes down to how much of a winner he feels like. Some of this has to do with him and his own emotional issues, and the rest is circumstantial.

Affairs usually start when a man feels misunderstood, like the areas of his life that are important to him are being criticized or deemed unimportant. Then he finds a woman who appreciates him, who gives him something he isn't getting from his primary relationship… and he strays. You can call him a pig or a jerk, but wouldn't it be more useful to try to understand why he did it, in this case because the thing closest to his heart has been ignored or neglected? The woman in his life isn't connecting with him in the way he wants most, and when that sort of pure appreciation comes from another source, he is understandably drawn to it.

For example, let's say a guy is a programmer. During the workday, he is on fire with passion and thrives on meeting the daily challenges of his job. After killing it all day, he comes home feeling on top of the world and wants to share that energy with his girl. She quickly dismisses him, saying, "You know I don't understand all that technical stuff, it just makes no sense to me. Can we talk about something else?" *Bam*, he has officially shut down. He feels like she doesn't accept the most important part of his life, the thing that makes him feel effective and worthwhile.

Since she doesn't care about what he does, he seeks that type of understanding elsewhere. He may spend more time with people who are part of that world, or are passionate about the same kind of mission. Maybe a girl will come along who finds what he does sexy, who appreciates him for the effort and passion he puts into it. When he's with her, he gets validation and appreciation for being the man he is and succeeding in the mission he's on. He feels good about himself around her, he feels seen, he feels desired… and these things combined have the potential to take him down a bad path.

You don't have to study code or take programming classes. It doesn't even matter if you're the most technologically challenged person on the planet. You don't have to connect with the technical side of it at all; what you should try to connect with are the *emotions* he expresses about it. It's easy to recognize when a man is excited about something, when he's driven to win and succeed. Try to tap into this vision of what he wants to make happen and connect with his passion.

I'm not saying cheating in this case is okay or acceptable. I'm not giving him an excuse, I'm just giving a reason. When my ex cheated on me, I was devastated and thought he was the world's biggest scumbag. I hated him and I hated her and I hated myself for getting involved with him and expending all my time and energy on him and the relationship. When some time had passed and I finally had the closure talk with him, there was no part of me that thought what he did was excusable, but I did finally understand *why* he did it. And it did give me some peace of mind (and maybe even restored my faith in men) to know that it wasn't a personal attack on me, that it didn't really have much to do with me at all; it was really about him and what he needed. He was miserable with me and he found happiness with her and though it did hurt a lot, I couldn't entirely blame him for jumping at the chance to be happy.

That relationship taught me many lessons, but the biggest of all was how essential it is to empower a man and *not* try to fix him. After that relationship, I never took ownership of a boyfriend's problems. If he was struggling with emotional issues or job stuff, I was supportive and encouraging, and being so often inspired him to get it together. We women really do have a lot of power at our disposal; we can run the show when it comes to inspiring a man and bringing out his best. We just need to know how to activate this power within ourselves.

## Make This Your Mantra

- A man's overall happiness and self-esteem are rooted in how much of a winner he feels like in the world. Men view the world in terms of whether they are getting closer to, or further from, their goals.
- The drive to win and conquer is hardwired into a man, and most men feel enormous pressure to succeed.
- In order for a man to feel truly alive and fulfilled, he needs to be pursuing his deepest aspiration and his "mission" in life. Your ultimate gift as a woman is to inspire him to do that — to realize his ultimate potential as a man.
- Love for a man is being with a woman who inspires him and makes him feel like a winner.

- A man wants to feel like he's the greatest thing that ever happened to you, like he will always be a winner when it comes to making you happy.

# Exercise

Try to discover your guy's mission:

- Notice his tone of voice and body language when he talks about certain things and observe what makes him light up and inspires him the most… then support and encourage him in those things.
- Ask him questions about his job, his passions, his goals in life. Even if you've been together for years, try to dig a little deeper into these areas and connect on a deeper emotional level to really understand what drives him.
- Ask him when he was the happiest and what he was doing at that point in time. Really listen to his answers.

# Resources

Check out the resource section for Chapter 3 (www.anewmode.com/resource) to delve deeper into the male psyche and better understand what it means for a man to feel like a winner.

Articles include:

Ask a Guy: How Can I Get Him to Treat Me Like a Priority?

What Every Man Wants in a Woman

How to Be a Great Girlfriend

Ask a Guy: He Lost His Job and Wants to Break Up

# Chapter 4: Men Are Terrified of Rejection

*"Love takes off the masks that we fear we cannot
live without and know that we cannot live within."*

~ *James Baldwin*

Ever like a guy and feel pretty confident he liked you back, and thought maybe he wasn't asking you out due to a fear of rejection? When in a relationship, have you noticed your guy suddenly become quiet, withdrawn, and uneasy, seemingly without cause or provocation?

Rejection hurts no matter what your gender, but it takes different forms for men and women. Given what we learned in the last chapter about how essential it is for a man to feel like a winner, it's not surprising that most men are absolutely terrified of rejection. Rejection is crushing for a man; it makes him feel like a worthless loser, and he will do anything to avoid it. Since men are usually the initiators when it comes to approaching women and asking them out, they have an extra hurdle to overcome. And because a man's sense of self is so tied to his ability to win, being rejected can have damaging consequences.

Rejection doesn't just mean he asks you out or asks for your number and you say no. A man can also experience rejection in the early stages of dating or in an established relationship, and even in marriage. The problem is, a lot of women don't know what rejection looks like to a man. When a man feels like a woman disapproves of him or is disappointed in him, he feels rejected. He feels not good enough, like a loser, like he has failed when he should have won.

# When You Know the Truth...

When you understand what rejection means to a man and how he experiences and processes it, it will shine a light on a whole new world. You will understand why he started losing interest, why he suddenly shut down, why he suddenly withdrew.

You will also know how to speak in a language he can really hear, and you will be able to reach him on the deepest, most significant level.

## Most Men Don't Feel Good Enough

When it comes to relationship fears, most women fear being unworthy of love while men typically fear not being good enough. A lot of men feel like their real self isn't good enough, that no woman will be able to love them for who they truly are. This is why a lot of guys are so afraid to let their guard down and face potential rejection. It's not that they're emotionally handicapped, it's that they are immensely vulnerable and protecting themselves from judgment and possible rejection.

Women often miss this because they're hypnotized by his "mask" – that is, the suave, cool, got-it-together appearance that the guy has on the surface. It's actually a huge mistake to engage with him on that surface level and believe that's who he really is.

In many ways, below that surface men feel alone in the world. They are conditioned by society to never show their emotions, so they downplay them. When a woman is intensely interested in who a man is, without preconceived expectations or judgment, he's able to rid himself of those underlying hesitations, open up and share himself. This is a pathway to intimacy with guys.

A lot of us don't realize how deeply insecure men can be about things we don't really understand. He may wear a mask of confidence, but deep down have fears of being incompetent, weak, unattractive, useless, or unintelligent. Men worry about not being able to provide for their woman and future family, not being what she wants, not being able to satisfy her sexually, not being able to be *the man*.

You can put some of these fears to rest by accepting him for who he is. He notices how you respond to him and the things he does for you. When you are never satisfied, it makes him fear that he'll never be good enough. When you truly appreciate him, those fears are alleviated and he feels capable of anything.

## Why Rejection Is the Bitterest Pill

Most men — even the ones who seem extremely confident on the outside — are terrified of being rejected. Rejection is such a miserable feeling that oftentimes a guy would rather avoid it and lose out on a potential opportunity than risk experiencing that pain.

As mentioned earlier, men need to feel like winners in the world. This is perhaps the most essential requirement in their lives. And nothing makes a man feel like more of a loser than being rejected by a girl. Rejection and failure are one in the same for most men.

Men cope with this in various ways. Some men act like cocky jerks and pretend they don't care... that way if they get rejected, they can rationalize that it's only because they were acting like jerks, and it wouldn't have happened had they been their true selves. It's like when you take a test and barely study and get a B. You feel pretty good about yourself and think if you had actually studied, you would have gotten an A for sure. Now if you did study really hard and you got a B, you probably wouldn't feel all that great about yourself.

Other men just don't try, because if you never try, you never fail. They may be aware they're missing opportunities, but this isn't enough to get them to overcome their overriding fear. Sometimes it can feel safer to not know and find comfort in your delusions, rather than face a crushing reality.

## Guy Confession

"Being brought down destroys us, and the feeling of being rejected is so crappy we would rather avoid it, even if that means losing a potential opportunity. If I'm out and see one girl in the room I'm interested in but think she'll reject me, I won't even bother, even if that means spending the whole night talking to girls I'm not interested in. The way I see it, if a girl likes me, she'll be drawn to me. If she isn't, then that means she probably isn't interested. I have a perception of myself that things typically just work out for me and I don't want to ruin that. So I don't make a move unless there's a high probability it will work out." - Kevin, 30

## Men Aren't Made of Steel

The stereotype about men and women is that men are strong and tough and women are sensitive and fragile. While this is definitely not a blanket statement, I think a lot of us internalize this idea. I think we women tend to think men are a lot tougher than they actually are, that they are immune to things like hurt feelings and criticism. It's understandable that women think this way because most men have been conditioned not to show their feelings publicly.

If a girl is rejected by a guy and feels hurt by it, she will cry to her friends and talk about her feelings. If a guy is rejected by a girl he will probably tell his friends, "Whatever, I wasn't that into her anyway," while inside he's really hurting and his self-esteem has suffered a major blow. He's not going to talk about it, though, so he will just suffer silently. Some guys will talk about it to those closest to them (I have many guy friends and hear it all the time), but it's not the norm.

I never really thought about it until I started writing about men. I, like many women, assumed men had egos built of steel that could withstand any rejection or insult. It's not the case, though. Men are also sensitive and emotional and vulnerable, and they too struggle with self-esteem issues and feeling worthy. Remember this when you turn a guy down or take a jab at him. Being in a happy, healthy, fulfilling relationship requires a certain degree of compassion and empathy (and as women, we're naturally pretty strong in these areas), so turn up the empathy a bit and don't think *He's a man, he can take it*, because that isn't always the case.

## When He's Afraid to Approach You...

*"Trying is just the first step toward failure."*

~ *Homer Simpson*

Remember in Chapter 1 how I told you that when a guy likes you, it's obvious? Well that is still very true, but it's important to mention that in the initial stages, his interest only becomes obvious once he thinks he has a shot... or at least when he isn't afraid that he'll be coldly rejected.

I interviewed many men before writing this book and asked them for the number one reason they might not approach a girl or ask her out when they're interested, and the answers were all exactly the same: fear of rejection.

For men, the negative feelings experienced from losing are a hundred times worse than any positive feelings experienced from winning. Most of the time the reward (you) isn't worth the risk (rejection). Compounding the problem is the fact that women are told not to show too much interest... to play coy, to be bitchy, to not show too much enthusiasm. While it's true that being too eager and desperate is a turnoff, coming off cold and bitchy is equally, if not more, man-repelling.

I had a friend like this once. Even though she was hot, she was the biggest man-repeller ever, to the point that my friends and I didn't want to invite her out with us. She just had this look in her eyes that told men: "If you approach me or my friends, I will cut you!" In fact, the night she met her boyfriend he was too afraid to come up and talk to her directly. Instead he asked *me* what her story was, and I was the go-between until he felt safe enough to approach. Maybe you think he was a wimp, but if you knew this girl you would understand!

Most girls don't realize how anxiety provoking it is for a man to just approach a girl and give it a shot. It can't be easy to constantly put yourself out there and risk rejection and feeling like a failure. When a man wants a woman and she rejects him, he feels that loss deeply. Throughout history, the men who were the biggest winners got access to the women. If a man couldn't go out and hunt and provide, then he wasn't a desirable mate. How this has evolved in modern times is that men look at how women respond to them almost as a measure of where they stand in terms of being either winners or losers in the world.

His fear of rejection doesn't need to be your problem, but you can make life easier by showing interest in a somewhat obvious way if you want him to ask you out. Guys don't pick up on nuances. If you're interested, playing coy and looking away or avoiding him won't encourage him to approach you; it will signal to him that you're *not* interested, and he'll move on.

Men aren't the only ones taking risks in this game of love. It can also be hard for us to put ourselves out there and express a little interest… because what if it doesn't get mirrored back at us? But as they say, without risk there is no reward.

You don't need to do anything bold or extravagant. If you see him checking you out, catch his eye and give him a smile. If he approaches and you get to talking, be happy, confident, and positive. Let him know (subtly) that he won't be shut down if he asks for your number or says he wants to take you out sometime.

That's really all you need to do. Show interest, maintain eye contact, be *happy*, and if he likes you, he'll take the bait and move things forward. If he doesn't, then he's not interested, and you should move on. Remember: When a guy likes you, it's obvious!

## Trying to Change Him: The Ultimate Rejection

*"A woman marries a man expecting he will change,*
*but he doesn't. A man marries a woman expecting*
*that she won't change, and she does."*

*~ Unknown*

I don't know why we do it… I don't know why we can't seem to help ourselves… but we gals always seem to be treating our guys like fix-it projects. Men can sense when a woman is trying to change or control them, and it isn't in the least bit motivating; it's crippling and defeating. It's basically telling a man that you reject him at his core; you want him to be someone else. It makes him feel like a failure, and as a result, he'll resist and retreat. In any relationship, it's imperative to accept the other person for who he is, the good and the bad. The worst thing you can do is to try to turn him into what you need him to be. It may sound crazy, but women do this all the time!

62

Inspiring someone to be his best self is not the same as changing him. Trying to change a man is an exercise in futility; you'll just end up disappointed and he'll feel resentful. You must take him as he is. This can be hard for many women since we have a natural caretaking instinct. A woman's default is to realize raw potential, that's why women are drawn to bad boys. They don't want him to stay bad, they want to be the one to extract the inherent goodness within him, turning him into the kind, sensitive soul he could be. All too often, women get caught up in turning a guy into what they want him to be, rather than accepting him as he is and encouraging him to become his best self.

People want to be seen, heard and appreciated for who they are. The worst feeling for pretty much anyone, but especially for guys, is the feeling that they aren't good enough. Yet this is the message you send when you try to change things about him. It can be anything from small things, like his appearance or table manners, to big things like wanting him to be something that goes against his nature, like more outgoing and charismatic even though he is a quiet, more subdued type.

You can't change someone's nature; you simply need to decide if you can accept him for who he is or not. You can encourage him to improve upon some of the small things, but it must be done in a kind, accepting way, not in the form of complaining, teasing, ridiculing, or constantly dropping not-so-subtle hints, all of which are insulting and emasculating.

You don't necessarily need to live with his unibrow or poor fashion choices forever, there are ways to encourage a few minor tweaks in a way that makes him feel good and want to do it. For instance, when he wears something that looks good, tell him he looks sexy. The best way to motivate a man is to be turned on by him. But at the end of the day, it's still his life. You may be a part of it, but he ultimately gets to decide how he wants to dress or cut his hair, how often he wants to go to the gym, how many eyebrows he wants to have, etc. There is a fine line between gently encouraging and turning into a nag, don't cross it.

If a man is going to change at all, it will be because he wants to, not because you're forcing him to. If he sees that doing certain things or looking a certain way makes you happy, he will most likely do those things or look that way, if he's already feeling like a winner in the relationship and doesn't sense you are rejecting him because he's not measuring up.

A lot of women will try to force change without trying to get to know a man at his core and showing appreciation and respect for who he truly is, and this usually backfires. It's also unnecessary, because when a guy feels appreciated and is starting to look at being with a woman long term, he will start to shape up on his own. He will take better care of himself, get his finances in order, and start being the man she wants him to be because he is ready and she didn't push him.

When you appreciate and accept him and have high expectations of him, he will usually rise up and be an even better man… but that won't change who he is at his core. If you can't accept certain things about him, don't waste time hoping these things will change. Instead, you need to decide if you can live with them or not.

A friend of mine got married at the age of 35 to a man she had been dating for about three years and living with for two. They got divorced a year later. Why? When they were a couple, he was lazy and would lie around on the couch all day not doing much of anything… then when they got married, he was lazy and would lie around on the couch all day not doing much of anything. Don't expect a man to suddenly change because he went from "boyfriend" to "husband." If you can't accept the way he chooses to live, he isn't the guy for you.

If you want him to improve in certain ways, you can gently encourage him, but don't push too hard if he isn't receptive. The more you do that, the more he'll feel like a loser, like you can't accept him, and like you wish he were someone else. This is the worst feeling in the world for a man, and the relationship will suffer greatly if he feels rejected in this way.

## Rejection in Committed Relationships

Rejecting a man doesn't just apply to the early courtship phases. Men can feel rejected in committed relationships as well... and it can hurt just as much if not more because it's with someone he's allowed himself to be vulnerable with. When you belittle him or knock down his ideas or his goals or his visions or even his appearance, *that* is a rejection. Men don't always distinguish between your rejecting something they said or did and your rejecting them as people.

## Personal Story

My mind works in a very linear way, and when I'm sharing a thought or idea, getting from point A to point B is all I see. I'm not as good at expressing myself verbally as I am at doing it in writing, so sometimes it takes a little while for me to make my point. If someone interjects in the middle, before I've finished forming what I was trying to say, I can't always process what they're saying and stop to consider it, because I'm still focused on what I was trying to express.

My husband's mind works very differently; to me he seems like he's all over the place because he doesn't need to go straight from point A to B, but instead can have a whole variety of thoughts and ideas all at once that spring from something minor. In the beginning, sharing my ideas with him could sometimes get challenging because before I could get to the main point of what I was trying to say, he would take things in an entirely different direction. Feeling frustrated, I would often quickly dismiss what he was saying as irrelevant because I wanted to get back to my point.

He later told me that the looks I gave him whenever he tried to contribute to the discussion in the way that was natural for him were crushing. He said I made him feel like what he was saying was of no value or substance, and sometimes like it was the dumbest thing I had ever heard, and it made him feel defeated. I'm glad he pointed it out to me, because I was able to work to correct the problem, and now we communicate and share ideas in a fun, healthy way. This is just one example of how a man can feel rejected in a committed relationship.

Just like we love it when men compliment us and show or tell us how much they cherish and adore us, men love it when we show that we respect and admire them for who they are and what they have to say. Making a guy feel like his insights are stupid or irrelevant crushes his spirit and makes him feel worthless. I never really got it until my current relationship, and it's been a valuable lesson. Once you learn it and internalize it, it will have a significant impact on both your life and relationships. Maybe there will be times you know more about a particular subject, or have more experience in a certain area, but it's still important to always respect someone else's opinion. This isn't just for men you're in a relationship with; it applies to people in general.

The fear of rejection that grips most men will usually stabilize when a man begins to believe he can bring something valuable to the world. This ties in closely to his need to feel like a winner; the more he feels like a winner, the less he fears rejection. Maybe he's the life of the party and really thrives in social settings. Maybe he's good at business, and people look to him for leadership and to make big decisions. A lot of a man's confidence is rooted in people looking to him for something.

As a woman, you have the power to find that something within him and draw it out. Try to notice areas where he wins (he may not always be aware of them) and point them out. Maybe he gives good advice, maybe he's amazing at reading people, maybe he has the ability to motivate and inspire the people around him, whatever it is that he provides that enhances the lives of those around him, notice and acknowledge it. When you do this, it gives him that "winner" feeling that turns every guy into a white knight. Don't zero in on the things he's not good at, the things he can't naturally provide, and point them out, because that will only make him feel rejected. If they are that important to you, then maybe this guy isn't your white night.

## Eric Confession

"A while back I was in a serious relationship with a woman I thought I was going to marry. I wasn't on much of a career track and was getting by working odd jobs and contract gigs. They weren't glamorous jobs, but they were easy and paid well. I had also been volunteering my time as a dating coach to men in Boston for roughly three years at that point. I had never told anyone in my life about my work as a dating coach — it was a bit of an odd job to begin with, and I figured people wouldn't understand.

I eventually did tell my girlfriend about my work and my dream to create a business devoted to helping people with their relationships. She loved the idea and told me she thought I would be outstanding at it. She said she could picture me writing a book one day and being tremendously successful. I remember being overwhelmed with a feeling of love and inspiration. To tell the truth, she believed in me more than I believed in myself.

I can't do it justice explaining it in print, but the inspiration she gave me in that moment changed my life. There was a flash inside my head and suddenly I felt like I really could have my dream … it was a magical moment for me, as corny as that sounds."

## Let's Talk About Sex (Specifically the Times You Don't Want to Have It…)

Another hot topic when it comes to men feeling rejected in relationships is rejection in the bedroom. In relationships, the man is usually the one who wants more sex. This isn't in *every* relationship, and many women love sex too, it's just that men usually want a bit more of it. A major complaint that men who are married or in long-term relationships have is not necessarily that their woman won't have sex as much as they want, it's the way she turns them down. There was even a spreadsheet that went viral not too long ago where a guy had written down all the excuses his wife used for not wanting to have sex over the course of seven weeks. It was pretty humorous, but also painfully true.

You don't need to have sex every single time he tries to initiate it. Sometimes you really are tired or have a headache or feel fat or just aren't in the mood. But you can turn him down in a way that shows him that you do desire him, that you are turned on by him, that you do want him… you just don't want to have sex right at that moment.

Every couple is different, so I won't give you a script for how to handle this; you know what to say to make your man feel loved and desired. Maybe you're annoyed that he wants so much sex, maybe you're exhausted and are frustrated that he's even trying. But relationships aren't only about our needs, they're about partnership and making each other feel loved and supported, so it's important to try to push past those reflexive feelings of annoyance and realize he's putting himself out there and risking rejection, and how you choose to respond will have an impact on your relationship.

# Make This Your Mantra

- For guys, the negative feelings experienced from losing are a hundred times worse than any positive feelings experienced from winning, and often it's not worth the risk.
- If there's a chance he'll be rejected, he may not even try. Fear of rejection is so much stronger than anticipation of reward.
- Guys don't pick up on nuances. If you want him to approach you, send a clear signal that tells him he won't be coldly rejected.
- Any time you disapprove of something a guy says or does, it feels like a rejection of who he is. The more insecure the guy, the more painful this will be.
- When you try to change him, the message he receives is that he's not good enough. When you try to change him, you are rejecting who he is and telling him he should be someone else.
- Men want to feel admired and desired by you. If they don't, they will feel rejected.

# Exercise

1. Next time you're out and a guy catches your eye, try not to look away the second he looks over at you. Instead, catch his gaze, give him a smile, and see what happens.
2. Show your guy pure acceptance and be mindful of the way you respond to him when you disapprove of something he says or does. (Be careful of eye rolling, an exasperated sigh, looking annoyed, using derogatory language, etc.)
3. Remember that disapproval is crushing for a man and can hurt almost on a physical level. Try to communicate with him from a place of patience and admiration.

# Resources

Visit our resource page (www.anewmode.com/resource) for more content on the topics covered in this chapter.

Articles in the section for Chapter 4 include:

Fool Proof Flirting Tips

How to Handle Rejection

How to Be More Approachable to Guys

Ask a Guy: Are Men Intimidated by "Strong Women"?

# Chapter 5: Men Want to Give and Make You Happy

*"Love is that condition in which the happiness of another person is essential to your own."*

*~ Robert Heinlein*

What do guys like in a girl? We get variations of this question all the time, and they usually go something like: How can I be a great girlfriend? What traits do men like in a woman? How do I make a man fall in love with me? What makes a woman irresistible? And on and on.

The underlying question here is actually quite simple. The only reason it gets confusing is because mainstream media focuses on everything *except* the main thing. We're told how to dress, how to style our hair, apply our makeup, what sex moves drive him wild, how to act… but no one really talks about the one thing that every man wants and needs in a woman, the thing that will determine whether or not he commits for life.

Men want a woman who can happily receive what they have to give.

Men are biologically wired to be providers. This dates back to the caveman days when men went out and hunted and brought home the bacon, as the saying goes. Times have obviously changed, and bacon can be acquired with a quick trip to the supermarket, but a man's inherent need to provide remains.

Being a provider doesn't mean he needs to make more money than you, or have a more prestigious job. It means he wants to provide for you in ways that will make you happy. This often has nothing to do with finances or material goods. It runs so deep that if a man doesn't feel like he can make a woman happy, he won't want to be in a relationship with her.

## When You Know the Truth...

You will be able to communicate with him in a way he hears and understands, in a way that motivates him to step up and be the man you want him to be. You won't feel constantly frustrated in your relationship, wondering how to get him to do the things — both big and small — that make you happy. You will know exactly what it takes to inspire him to bring his best to the relationship.

If you're single, you will know what areas to work on in order to finally attract the kind of guy and kind of love you've always wanted.

## When a Woman Can Happily Receive

*"We tend to forget that happiness doesn't come as a result of getting something we don't have, but rather of recognizing and appreciating what we do have."*

*~ Frederick Koenig*

Men want to feel manly and significant. They want to provide for you, it's just in their nature to be that way. However, a man will only want to give to a woman who can happily receive what he has to offer, not one who is going to make unnecessary demands in order to feel good about herself and secure in the relationship.

A man must feel like he can make a woman happy before he bonds. He doesn't want or expect you to give him anything back; he wants to see how well you can receive what he gives.

This ties into a man's need to feel significant. He wants to feel like he has something to offer you, like he can enhance your life in some positive way. *This* is what ignites a man's interest and causes him to invest in a woman and in a relationship.

It's not about your needing something from him because you're helpless and need a man to rescue you, it's about him feeling like he can bring something into this world that is of value, both in the relationship and independent of it.

This idea has become completely twisted in today's world, and many women think men will feel threatened or intimidated by them if they earn more money or have a more successful career.

Most men don't care if you have a higher education or make more money. Most guys realize that they could go for a higher degree if they wanted and needed to, and no man gets into a relationship to be the one making more money. Men enter into relationships when the time spent with the other person creates something better and greater than he could ever have on his own. It's not about being "more than" the other person; it's about fitting together and creating a meaningful partnership.

In this day and age, women don't need a man to provide financial security. Women can earn as much as men and get advanced degrees. And women are becoming increasingly more prominent in the realm of business and education. In decades past, women didn't have these opportunities, and marriage for a woman was more about necessity and survival than love and romance. A man felt significant because he was the sole provider, and a woman would put up with some of his weaker points because she needed him and didn't have much of a choice. Fortunately, this is no longer the world we live in. Yet men still need to feel like they have something of value to offer you.

Both men and women can have deep-seated insecurities, but these insecurities have different root causes. Women primarily feel insecure about their physical appearance, while men feel insecure about their ability to have an impact on the world. In a relationship, feeling powerless and useless to a man is the equivalent of feeling unattractive and undesirable for a woman.

Men don't feel emasculated because women can provide for themselves or because they make more money. A man feels emasculated when his girl is disappointed with the person he is and wants him to be different. It could be that she doesn't accept his job, his passions, certain elements of his personality, or the way he navigates the world. Being a woman who receives what a man has to offer can be subtler than you think. Sometimes it's as simple as being present and engaged while he tells you about his day, or simply laughing at his joke. Men want to feel wanted, and they are not going to stay in a relationship when they don't. This has nothing to do with income levels; being receptive to a man is about appreciating and enjoying him for who he is.

If a woman is well educated and highly successful and she disapproves of her man because he isn't at her level in those areas, that's when success becomes a problem. If she doesn't consider him her equal, she won't be receptive to what he has to offer because it will never be enough. The problem here is that she feels superior, and he knows it. A successful woman who fully accepts her man and is with him because she thinks he's awesome and amazing, and because to her, he's "the man," sidesteps this issue completely. When a woman happily receives what her man has to offer, her success is a non-issue, both for her and for him.

## Personal Story

I'll admit there was a point in my life when I adopted the attitude "I don't need anything from anyone." I had been burned so many times that I decided to pour my life into my career and be great at that. I still dated, but I was jaded and me-centered and very set on maintaining an iron façade and showing no weakness… lest I get hurt once again. It's not that I would brag about my accomplishments on dates, but the conversations did tend to focus on my career, my goals, my drive. I didn't even really care about what the guy had to say — a date for me at that point in time was more of an opportunity to show off how truly fabulous and independent I was.

To my confusion, a lot of the guys I dated didn't want to continue dating me… even the ones who, to be perfectly honest, should have been grateful I gave them a chance to begin with! I decided to approach it as a learning opportunity and find out why, and so I asked some of them straight out. The answers I got from the guys were pretty consistent. They basically felt that someone like me wouldn't be able to respect them… that I would make them feel inadequate… that they didn't feel they could measure up to my standards… that they weren't as accomplished as I was. At first I took this to mean my career was hindering my chances of finding love, but in time I realized something else was at play. My years of living like a lone ranger had me feeling very disconnected and pretty lonely, so I shifted my mentality and began to realize that it's okay to let people in. In fact, it could be kind of nice.

Even though I had found even *greater* career success at this point in time, not one guy I dated felt threatened or intimidated by me. The problem wasn't my success, it was my "I don't need anything from anyone" mentality. Men do not like neediness, but they do, to an extent, want to feel needed. When I say needed I mean necessary. He doesn't want to feel like an ornament, but rather a vital part of your life, someone who can enhance it.

# When You Acknowledge What He Has to Offer...

For a man to really feel good about himself in a relationship, he needs to be with a woman who sees what he has to offer and appreciates it. Maybe he gives great advice, maybe he's a good listener, maybe he has a sharp wit, maybe he notices things that most people miss, maybe he's creative — whatever it is, he wants a woman who sees the value in it. He wants to be able to share his strengths in a way that makes her life better and happier.

It's important to let him know how valuable he is to you. A guy doesn't always make the connection that being in his presence makes you feel better. He doesn't always realize how much you value having him around and in your life. He doesn't know he's making your life a better place just by being in it.

A man's greatest concern in a relationship is not being able to make a woman happy, being a disappointment. So he tries to do what he can, and he doesn't always know when he's getting it right. Don't assume he already knows... *tell him*. Make him realize you appreciate what he brings to the table. When he becomes aware of it, and sees how much you appreciate him, your relationship will flourish.

None of this can happen if you're coming from a place of fear, though. It's not about creating a sense of security because you're afraid he'll leave or lose interest. It's not about making him be a certain way to alleviate your fears and worries. It's about building a genuine connection and seeing what he has to offer and drawing it out of him so he becomes his best self (this will also bring out the best in you). *This* is what creates healthy relationships. It's not about how often he texts or when you sleep together or about following any sort of rules to capture a man's heart. Relationships are about creating a meaningful connection and seeing if two people fit together in a way that can lead to a solid, lifelong partnership.

## Spell It Out for Him

Now that we've covered why it's important for a man to feel like he can make you happy, let's get specific and talk about how you can communicate your needs to him in a way that inspires him to meet them. Being direct and telling him outright what you want and what makes you happy goes a long way. I know it isn't ideal; we would rather he just *know*, but that isn't a fair or realistic expectation. Guys want to make you happy and they appreciate it when you express your wishes clearly.

A lot of women write to Eric and me about frustrations in their relationship — he doesn't call or text enough, he's not romantic like he used to be, he doesn't show enough affection, he doesn't help out around the house. They'll say: "I tell him over and over that this is what I want him to do, and he still doesn't do it! Why is he so difficult?!"

It's not what you say, it's the *way* you say it. When you come at a man from a blaming or accusatory place, he will automatically shut down. But when you approach him from a place of love and compassion, he will rise up and *want* to do whatever you ask and more. Basically, it has to come from the right place and be said in the right way. Saying, "I love it when you call me in the middle of the day just to say hi," will get you your desired result much faster than saying, "Why don't you ever call me just to say hi?" The latter will make him feel like he's failing you, and he will be less motivated to try. It's just natural for a man to react that way. When he feels defeated, he retreats.

Most women don't realize that men need things spelled out in clear, straightforward terms. Men are not as good at picking up on hints and nuances as women are. If you want him to do something, just tell him directly in a kind and loving way. No blaming, no shaming, no guilt-tripping, just be open and direct. *That's it!*

Nagging is the number one way *not* to get what you want. Instead, it stirs up his defenses and causes him to feel like a failure. It makes him feel like he can't do anything right and kills any motivation he may have had to try.

A lot of women know this and in an effort not to come across like a nag, they resort to making a different major mistake: dropping hints and then getting angry when he doesn't pick up on them. While the guy has no idea anything is amiss, you feel a silent fury building inside... *How can he not know this is what I want?! He should realize this would make me happy! He should know this — I shouldn't have to say anything!* And the resentment builds. When he asks what's wrong, you say "nothing," because you don't want to nag, and he takes that to mean nothing is wrong because men are pretty literal creatures. But you become even angrier... *How can he not know that I'm upset about this?!* He feels your punishing energy and doesn't know how to deal with it, so he retreats. This makes you even more upset, and the cycle continues.

If you want him to do something, don't drop hints and expect him to understand exactly what you want. That is an unfair expectation to have of anyone.

Trust me, I know how special it makes you feel when he does exactly what you want without you having so say a word, but it just isn't realistic to expect him to get it right every single time.

So what should you do?

Communicate in a clear and direct way and reward him when he does something you want. The more he feels like he's "winning" at making you happy, the more he'll try to find ways to keep doing more. So let's say you come home after a long day and want to talk to him about a stressful issue that came up at work. If he gives you his full attention, say: "Thank you so much for listening. I really appreciate it," followed by a soft caress or a kiss, anything that will feel good to him. If he doesn't give you his full attention and is distracted by his phone or the TV, just nicely ask him if he could give you a few minutes of his focused attention, and then thank him and reward him for it.

As another example, let's say he doesn't call or text you during the day and this bothers you. Saying "I love it when you text me randomly during the day," will get you much further than: "Why don't you ever call or text me?! It takes two seconds and I know you have your phone with you at all times!" In the first example, you are expressing your love for him. You are letting him know he means a lot to you and it makes you happy to hear from him. In the second, you are accusing him and essentially telling him he better do what you want, or he will suffer for it.

Trust me, I know how tempting it is to begin a sentence with "You never..." or "Why don't you ever..." but those never result in a healthy exchange. Starting off with "I love it when you..." or "It makes me feel so good when you..." may not always be easy, but it gets you results!

Another important thing to remember is to leave the issue alone once you've discussed it. Once you voice what you want, give him time to do it and just silently expect that he will. A lot of women will stay upset after telling their men what they want and continue to stress out over it. For example, let's say you tell your guy that you want him to take you out on dates more often, and you do it in a nice, loving way. If you don't expect that he will meet your needs, you will continue to stress out over it and get more upset with each passing day that he hasn't immediately arranged a romantic date (even though it could well have to do with busy schedules or something else, and not him ignoring your needs). I know I've made this mistake more than once in the past, and I know when I did it was always because of my own insecurities.

Instead of worrying that he won't do something, just leave it alone after you bring it up; put it out of your mind. If nothing has changed in about two weeks, then maybe bring it up again and see if you can work together to find a solution so that you both feel happy. You could also take the initiative and suggest a restaurant or activity and then afterward let him know how much fun you had, and how connected you feel to him when you do fun activities together. This is *so* much better that feeling angry and hurt, stewing in resentment, and passive-aggressively punishing him for it until you can't hold back anymore and launch into him with an angry tirade.

The worst way to encourage a man to do anything is to harp on him or nag him about it or make him feel bad or guilty. Remember, men need to feel like winners. If you are constantly telling him what he's doing wrong and how he is essentially failing you, he will feel dejected and won't bother trying anymore. When you tell him what you want in a way that is encouraging — not in a way that's accusatory, demanding, or nagging — he feels inspired to go above and beyond.

Appreciation is catnip to a man, so don't skimp on showing or telling him how happy it makes you when he does what you want him to. Nothing is more attractive and appealing to a man than a woman who is thoroughly happy with him and appreciates him. When he sees he can make you happy, he will be motivated to do whatever he can to keep you that way. Your body is the ultimate reward center. When he does something that makes you happy, reward him through your touch, your voice, your eyes, and especially your smile.

## Guy Confession

"Girls have to be patient. Men are dumb, we're oblivious, we're not always in tune to a girl's feelings. It's not because we don't want to be, we do want to be, we just need guidance. Tell me where to go and I'll take you there. I don't need a girl to make it happen, I can do that. I just need some direction sometimes, and for her to tell me how she feels and what she wants, and I'll do whatever I can to give it to her. I may screw up, and when I do I appreciate it when the girl doesn't punish me for it and is understanding and takes those errors with a grain of salt. Winning a guy over really comes down to patience, understanding, and good communication." - Jason, 28

## Men Want a Happy Woman

Most men feel bogged down by daily demands. Life is tough, and navigating its waters can be difficult. What every man wants is a woman who is happy and pleasant to be around. Men love putting a smile on your face and knowing they were the cause of it. When you continually deny him that success in making you happy, he gives up.

This does *not* mean you aren't allowed to be unhappy, have your own issues, or experience and express unpleasant emotions. You are not a robot. But there is a way to express your unhappiness that can bring about resolution, and there is a way to do it that can bring about dissolution. It's a matter of mindset and approach. A woman in a good place can openly and honestly express what she needs. A woman in a bad place can only demand that her man give her certain things, and punish him if he doesn't.

The way you convey your feelings is usually determined by how you feel about yourself and your relationship. If you feel insecure, or don't fully trust that he loves you and is committed to you, then you will have expectations and make demands in order to feel more secure. But he won't ever be able to give you that sense of inner peace, it doesn't matter how much he does for you. He can text you back promptly nine times out of ten, and you'll use that one time when he took too long as proof he doesn't care or is losing interest.

Coming from a place where you feel secure and confident in your relationship looks completely different (even if you're asking for the exact same thing). When you are secure and trust that he loves you, you want certain things from him because you want to build upon, and deepen, your connection. This isn't the same as needing him to do things in order for you to feel validated.

The desire to be present and invested in a relationship is ignited in a guy when the woman is happy. When a woman is happy, at ease, and not looking to get certain things from the relationship in order to feel validated, she emits a positive vibe that is irresistible to a guy.

## Personal Story

The age of 22 marks a transitional time for most, and it was a time when I changed dramatically... and not for the better. I had graduated from college feeling hopeful and optimistic about my future. I was going to get a job at a leading women's magazine and quickly climb up the ranks, and soon I would be a published author and everything would be fabulous! It was around this time that I met Dean. He was smart and cute and charming, and being two years older he was a bit more settled in his life. He was smitten with me right from the start and told me early on that I was the kind of woman he could see himself marrying. A promising start, indeed.

During the course of our relationship, my idealism gave way to reality. I was going on countless job interviews and getting nowhere. After a few months, I ended up taking an unpaid internship working in the closet of a fashion department at a magazine. The hours were long and the job was thankless. I picked up another no-pay internship and started writing a weekly fashion column for a start-up site — the one job I actually got paid for! I was working about 18 hours a day and making $25 a week.

At first I was optimistic that all these hours of experience would lead to an amazing job with an actual salary, but as the months rolled by, I found myself bitter, angry, and jaded. I barely had time to eat and literally dropped 15 pounds in a matter of weeks. Dean tried to be supportive, but any time he said or did anything, I would bite his head off. And when I did manage to find some free time to spend with him, I spent the entire time venting about how stressed out I was and how awful the fashion industry was.

The relationship was deteriorating fast, but I was too wrapped up in my own life to notice. Then he disappeared. I didn't hear from him for an entire week. My calls and texts went unanswered, and I was puzzled. When I did finally get him on the phone, he sounded cold and distant. He told me that I had changed and he didn't want to continue the relationship. "You moved to the city, started working in fashion, lost all this weight, and now you're someone I don't even recognize. You used to be so fun and nice, and now you're bitter and mean. I have a tough life, too — my job is stressful, I just moved into a new apartment, I'm struggling to stay afloat — and you don't even notice or care. I can't be with someone like that, and your energy is just poison to be around."

I couldn't even argue with him because he was right. I had a bunch of his stuff that he'd left at my apartment, including about five designer ties from the likes of Gucci and Burberry. I asked when he wanted to pick them up and he said he didn't, to just throw everything out. Was he being dramatic? Maybe a tad, but *that's* how much he never wanted to see me and my toxic energy again!

I wish this incident had been a bigger wake-up call, but I didn't start to actively choose happiness until years later. I felt bad about the way I'd acted and was a much nicer person in my next relationship, but I still operated under the belief that happiness would somehow find me… as soon as I had the right job… the right apartment… the right wardrobe… the right boyfriend… then it would happen. This is not how happiness works. I essentially used my relationship as an emotional dumping ground. The reason I shared this not-so-flattering story is to demonstrate just how repulsive an unhappy woman really is, because I'm telling you, those were some really nice ties!

## It's Not His Job to Make You Happy

*"It is not easy to find happiness in ourselves, and it is not possible to find it elsewhere."*

~ *Agnes Repplier*

Although men love making a woman happy and doing so gives them the greatest satisfaction they can feel in a relationship, men are not responsible for your happiness in this world. Happiness isn't owed to you, and it doesn't come from your relationship. You create your own sense of happiness and fulfillment. If you don't feel good about yourself or your life, nothing he does will ever penetrate. This is where most relationship problems develop. She feels unhappy and thinks it's his job to make her happy, and he feels frustrated because nothing he does is enough.

If you feel unhappy or dissatisfied about something in your relationship, first look within yourself and see if it is a manifestation of some deeper issue or insecurity.

84

For instance, women who have been burned in the past (which is most of us) may out of fear project certain negative intentions onto their current partner that he doesn't deserve. Maybe your ex left you for someone else, or just dumped you out of the blue. Even though you know that your current guy isn't your ex, and this is a new relationship, a part of you may be on the lookout for signs that history will repeat itself. So you look to your guy to give you reassurance. If one day he isn't as loving or attentive as usual, you panic and think he's losing interest, and you don't let go of it until you get some sign that shows he still cares. When the validation comes, your fears are temporarily alleviated and you feel a sense of relief... but then a few days later he seems a bit distant and those fears erupt all over again.

If you find that you constantly need him to tell you he loves you or be affectionate or compliment you, ask *why* you need these things. Is it because of your own fears, or do you genuinely not feel as secure and connected to him as you would like to be? If your need doesn't have a deeper psychological cause and is coming from a genuine place of wanting to deepen your relationship, then you can discuss the issue with him. Again, make sure you have clarity first and can come from a place of caring and compassion. And if you are struggling with trust issues stemming from the past, share that with him. This is much healthier than blaming him or expecting him to be a certain way. If you can tell him where you're coming from, he will probably feel even more bonded to you and will have a deeper understanding of who you are.

## Happiness Is From Within

*"Nothing can bring you happiness but yourself."*

*~ Ralph Waldo Emerson*

Happiness isn't something that happens. And it doesn't come from external sources. It is something you seek and build within yourself and allow to flow outward and into your relationship. It comes from how you relate to life, not from your relationship. If you believe that a man holds the key to your happiness, you are laying the groundwork for difficult relationships and chronic dissatisfaction.

Dealing with and overcoming the pains of the past will take more work for some than others. It could come from journaling about your feelings and identifying a root cause of certain issues, or it may require talking to a good therapist. No matter what you've been through in life, make an effort to work through anything that is holding you back from getting what you want in life. Your past doesn't have to continue to define you; it is possible to break free and move forward.

Aside from healing inner wounds, an essential part of maintaining happiness is to keep doing things that bring you happiness outside of your relationship. A lot of us make the mistake of letting things fall by the wayside as soon as we're in a relationship. We don't go to the gym as often, don't go to book club, abandon hobbies, don't make time to spend with friends. When you no longer have these sources of happiness, you develop a void that the relationship must fill. This places way too much pressure on the relationship. The purpose of being in a relationship is not to fill a void in your life. Relationships aren't about getting, they're about giving, sharing, and experiencing.

One person can't fulfill your every need. I know you want to spend all your time with him; maybe you even think it's selfish of you to sometimes choose other activities over time spent with your significant other, but it is *essential*. When your life is no longer well-rounded and fulfilling, you will be off balance internally and this will create a negative vibe that can poison your relationship. When you make having a life outside of your relationship a priority, your relationship will automatically improve.

Remember, *you* control your thoughts, *you* control how you spend your time, and *you* control how happy you are.

## Make This Your Mantra

- Men want a woman who can happily receive what they have to give.
- He wants to feel like the best thing that's ever happened to you; let him know as often as possible all the ways he is enriching your life.
- If a man doesn't feel like he can make a woman happy, he won't want to be in a relationship with her.
- A man loves putting a smile on your face and knowing he was the cause of it. When you continually deny him that success in making you happy, he gives up.
- Your level of happiness is under your control; take ownership of it and fill your life with things that make you happy.

## Exercise

Keep a gratitude journal:

- If you're single, write down two things you're grateful for in your life every day (and you can't repeat the same things twice).
- If you're in a relationship, you should do this as well, making sure to write down two things that have nothing to do with your man or your relationship, to ensure you are expecting and seeking happiness in the life you're living, not expecting your man or your relationship to provide happiness for you.
- If you're in a relationship, you can also write down two things you appreciate about your man each day (you can choose to share it with him or keep it to yourself). Doing this will put your mind into a more positive space and help you naturally radiate happiness and positivity, enhancing your life in numerous ways.

# Resources

Learn more about how your level of happiness impacts your relationship and how to find true happiness within yourself in the section for Chapter 5, found at www.anewmode.com/resource.

Articles include:

Ask a Guy: When a Man Loves You...

10 Things Confident People Do Differently in Relationships

11 Ways to Find True Happiness

How to Be an Amazing Girlfriend

6 Guaranteed Ways to Be Miserable

# Chapter 6: Men Are Afraid of Losing Their Freedom

*"Freedom is not the absence of commitments, but the ability to choose — and commit myself to — what is best for me."*

~ Paulo Coelho, The Zahir

Men are afraid of losing their freedom. This is true. The misconception that gets perpetuated, though, is that men hate commitment, are anti-relationship, and just want to run wild and do whatever they want. This isn't actually the case. Freedom for a man is more of a psychological state than having the *actual* freedom to run around and do whatever he wants. No one talks about this, though. Instead, books and articles are written giving women a playbook to trap a man into commitment. They paint a picture that looks a lot like the coyote chasing after the roadrunner.

As a result of all this misinformation being perpetuated in the mainstream, a lot of women focus on the wrong things. They worry that their guy isn't serious, that he'll never commit, that he doesn't see a future… and they panic, wondering what they can do to beat the odds and get a man to do the impossible… commit! But it isn't impossible. It also doesn't require following a set of rules or only saying and doing certain things, because *men also want commitment.*

Again, it comes down to winning and losing. If a man believes he is winning in the relationship more than he ever could on his own, then he will commit. If he feels as though being in the relationship shuts down his ability to win (and *feel* like a winner) and that he would have an easier time outside the relationship, then that's when commitment becomes an issue. That's when he shuts down and doesn't want to move forward.

## When You Know the Truth...

You won't panic over the state of your relationship... you will be able to be *in* the relationship and know exactly how to give him what he wants and needs. You won't strategize or plot or scheme, you will just know. Being too eager or available isn't the problem; *fear* is the problem. Like the fear that men are afraid of commitment and the only way to get a man to commit is to trick him into it. When you know the truth, you will be free to be yourself, you will know what it takes to really reach a man, and you will put any fears he may have to rest.

## What Is Freedom in a Relationship?

*"You must love in such a way that the person you love feels free."*

~ *Thich Nhat Hanh*

Having freedom is not about him wanting to go out and sleep with hundreds of women, it's about him not wanting to feel trapped in a situation where he has to be a certain way or else his partner will punish him for it.

Men are not afraid of relationships. What men are afraid of is being stuck in a *bad* relationship. Most men really do enjoy being in relationships (when it's with the right woman, that is), but at the same time, most men have a huge fear of getting trapped in a situation with a woman who sucks them dry and leaves them feeling drained and uninspired. A man will feel "free" in a relationship when he's with a woman who is whole and fulfilled in her life and doesn't rely on him and the relationship to meet her every need.

For example, let's say he is feeling off balance and wants to take some time for himself to recalibrate and get back into a good place. He needs to recharge in order to be the best man he can be in the relationship. His girlfriend doesn't see it this way, though, and gets on his case for not being as attentive as she would like. This causes him to feel even more stressed out and even more pressured, and he may start to resent her and back away even more.

A man doesn't want to feel like he can't do the things he needs to do for his well-being, lest he get reamed out for it. This isn't to say he wants to come and go as he pleases, in and out of the relationship. But sometimes he may need certain things, such as space, in order to get himself into a good place. What he wants is a woman who will understand and accept that. A guy needing space doesn't look like him going out and flirting with girls in a bar; what it really comes down to is him knowing that if he needs a weekend to play video games or just zone out and shut himself off, she will be okay. She won't take it personally, she won't think it means he doesn't care, she won't ask why he's pulling away or tell him he "should" talk to her if something is wrong or he "should" want to spend time with her, she'll just accept that this is what he needs, and that's that. *That* is freedom to a man.

When a guy feels like he can't do the things he wants and needs to do because it will make you upset or angry, that's when he feels trapped.

If you felt like you couldn't do the things you needed to do, if doing them came with painful consequences and caused worse problems, you would probably feel suffocated and come to resent the person holding the figurative pillow. This is how it feels for guys.

Couples who give each other space when needed and can communicate openly, without fear of being blamed or shamed for expressing their needs, become closer. Couples who can't do this are susceptible to constant fights and a tension-filled relationship.

This really gets to the heart of why men are extremely drawn to confident, secure women who have their own lives. When a woman has her own life, he knows she won't rely on him to fill an emotional void. She also won't discourage him from living his life and doing what he needs to do to be the man he wants to be and to fulfill his potential.

## When a Man Needs Space

*"Men want the same thing from their underwear that they want from women: a little bit of support, and a little bit of freedom."*

*~ Jerry Seinfeld*

It may seem counterintuitive, but sometimes a little bit of space is the most effective way to get even closer.

A lot of women have a hard time understanding why their men are suddenly withdrawing emotionally. In their frustration, they may make the problem even worse. A guy can pull back for several reasons. Usually it's not a conscious thing; it can be an automatic response when he feels stressed out or emotionally overwhelmed. Sometimes this can be the result of something in the relationship, but sometimes it has nothing to do with the relationship at all.

The worst thing a woman can do is take it personally and see herself as the problem. If she gets angry with him for not talking to her about what's going on, he feels even more pressured and she becomes another problem he needs to deal with.

This isn't easy for most women to understand and accept because it's just not our process. When we're upset, we seek the people closest to us for support. We want to confront the problem, talk about it, and deal with it, not separate ourselves from it. Men are not like this. When a man is feeling unbalanced, he needs to retreat and work through it on his own. Instead of realizing that needing space is about him, we make it about us and think he doesn't feel close to us or is shutting us out. Rather than seeing that this is what will enable him to function optimally in the relationship, we often take it to mean he doesn't care about the relationship. We all view reality through our subjective experiences, and typically when a woman pulls back or neglects someone, she does it for a clear reason and to send a strong message.

So when a guy starts spending more time with friends, more time absorbed in other activities and projects, a woman might take it to mean she did something wrong to push him away and go into fix-it mode, analyzing what she may have done wrong and doing whatever she can to bring him closer, which is the opposite of what he needs. This will likely result in him pulling back even more, followed by her pushing more, on a continuous loop, solving nothing and creating even more problems.

If you allow your fears to dominate your objective reasoning, you may start acting overly needy or demanding. Or maybe you won't say anything at all, but will silently resent him for taking the space he needed and begin withholding your love and affection.

It's hard to be objective when our feelings are involved. On one hand, you may know that this is how men deal with things (and most of us are well versed on what a physical and emotional "man cave" is), but on the other hand you still feel hurt by it. As much as I've written about this topic, as much as I've dished out this advice, even *I* have a hard time with this one on occasion. I too can let my ego and my emotions get involved, and even though I truly know that it has nothing to do with me… it just *feels* like it has something to do with me. It takes practice and understanding, and these things don't always come easy. The best strategy is to just remind yourself that it has nothing to do with you; it's just how he processes things.

When you interpret his behavior as him "not caring" or "not putting the relationship first," and try to force him to go back to the way he was before, you're not accepting him for who he is, and you will end up chasing a static and unrealistic version of the relationship and sucking the life out of it. You will create a pressure-filled vibe that makes him want to retreat even further.

---

## Is he losing interest?

## Take our QUIZ to find out the truth!
**www.anewmode.com/losing-interest-quiz**

---

The thing is, he never stopped caring. He was just trying to recharge so he could be his best self in the relationship. When he starts feeling smothered and suffocated, he thinks, "Why can't she let me have my own life and do what I *love*?" and he may start to resent you for not letting him be.

When you interrupt his process and worry about what him needing space means, thinking it's all about you, you will do tremendous damage to the relationship because you will be denying him something that he *needs*. Men know that it isn't easy or natural for women to step back, so if you can manage to do it, he will notice and appreciate it and will come to love you even more.

# Eric Confession

"I can tell you firsthand that when people try to probe into why I am being distant, it feels very invasive to me and I withdraw even further. That doesn't mean I think the person "probing" is a bad person or that they have bad intentions. It's more that I don't want to feel exposed and vulnerable while I'm already in pain. All I want is to quietly solve the problem by myself. I don't want to be coddled. I don't want to be reassured. And I definitely don't want to be pitied. I do want the woman I'm with to be okay, though; I don't want her to worry or be upset. And I don't want her to see me as anything less than the man I aspire to be — the man that I am when I'm at my best. So with all that in mind, you could sum it up by saying: I want her to give me space and I want her to be okay while she's giving me space."

# When a Woman Gets Clingy

*"Immature love says: 'I love you because I need you.' Mature love says: 'I need you because I love you.'"*

~ *Erich Fromm*

Neediness is a word that gets thrown around a lot when it comes to relationship issues, but there's a lot of confusion about what it actually is.

Neediness is a mindset more than a set of behaviors. When a woman is needy, she isn't receptive to what a man gives her because she's always desperate for more. And a part of her doesn't really trust that she will get what she needs, so instead of enjoying and appreciating what she *is* receiving, she's fixated on what she's *not* receiving and why. When a man feels like nothing he does is enough, he feels defeated and stops trying. The needy person uses this as proof that she's unworthy, and it fuels her insecurities even more. She acts even more needy as a result, pushing him further and further away.

The sad fact is, most people are *starving* to connect in a real and genuine way. They want to be their authentic selves and feel loved for who they are. They want to be supported by someone who is their partner. At the same time, they are terrified that they don't really deserve these things, or that it won't work out and they will be destroyed. Even still, the need to connect is so strong that when the prospect of a relationship or deeper connection presents itself, men and women who are starving for it end up acting desperately and clinging to the relationship as if it's the one and only source of joy in their life… and maybe it is.

Clinginess can be subtle. It doesn't have to mean you are constantly nagging him and whining about things. It could be you getting upset over small things, like him not being 100% loving and affectionate at all times. Sometimes something as small as him not texting you back for a few hours, or not ending the conversation by saying "I love you" can set you off and make you feel like he doesn't really care. When enough of these things happen, you will start to feel really bad in the relationship and may blame your guy for making you feel that way. From there, a poisonous mindset can form, a mindset that says: "If I'm not happy or not okay, it's your responsibility to make it better because we're in a relationship." You don't need to say it outright, it will seep into all of your interactions with him and will activate his defenses. He will resent being in charge of your emotional well-being and will start to feel like he's walking on eggshells, like he can't do the things he needs and wants to do because it might make you hurt or angry or upset, and it's just not worth it to him. To avoid this, he does what you want him to do, but he does it because he has to, not because he wants to. When he has the choice, he'll choose you. When he has no choice, he may do what you want, but he'll do it grudgingly.

Essentially, the needy state of mind is when you believe that you *need* the relationship to be a certain way to *make you happy* or *make you feel okay* or *make you feel complete* or *make you feel significant*. The needy mindset happens when you believe that your emotional state is determined by what happens in the relationship. You have the belief that this other person holds the keys to your emotional well-being, as it relates to your happiness, a sense of relief, a sense of wholeness, a sense of significance, self-esteem, and so forth.

If you haven't noticed or been here yourself (most of us have), an insecure person's need for constant approval is exhausting. And we all intuitively pick up on someone's insecurities. They don't even need to say anything in particular; it just lingers in the air.

## Getting to the Heart of the Matter

*"I do not trust people who don't love themselves and yet tell me, 'I love you.' There is an African saying which is: Be careful when a naked person offers you a shirt."*

*~ Maya Angelou*

A lot of people make the mistake of believing that a relationship will give them the confidence and fulfillment they've been seeking. They may see problems in their lives, but assume that finding the right man will render those issues null and void. It's not our fault; just look at the way love is portrayed in the media! *Love is all you need, love is the answer, you complete me, and they lived happily ever after...* we've been saturated with false representations of love for most of our lives.

This skewed perception of love and the mindset this perception creates usually leads a girl to seek validation from her relationship, rather than from within. If her significant other doesn't call or text, she panics, thinking he no longer loves her (and therefore she is no longer lovable). She will desperately try to get assurance from him by any means necessary. She may read into every little thing he says or does, looking for reassurance that he cares about her, or fixating on signs he may not.

This dynamic most often stems from a lack of self-esteem and the belief that she is unworthy of love, resulting in a cycle of trying to quiet that voice telling her she is unworthy by finding evidence that he does care (and therefore she is worthy). But any evidence she finds that he does care doesn't stand a chance against the evidence that he doesn't, since she's biased toward believing she is unworthy to begin with, thus making evidence of that stronger and more dominating. She can never feel relaxed in the relationship because she is always on high alert, waiting for it all to implode. And in the midst of this anxiety, she can't just *be*. She can't enjoy what she has, because all she sees is what she stands to lose.

There are books that will tell you to be coy, to make him wait a certain amount of time before responding to a text, to not accept dates unless he makes them three days in advance. There are an assortment of other tips about how to behave so you appear confident and not needy. These tactics may treat the symptoms to an extent, but they don't cure the disease. The fundamental issue has nothing to do with how you behave, per se; it has to do with what your mindset is. It's an issue that comes from not feeling okay and outsourcing your okay-ness to him.

It's not a matter of you wanting to be around him or with him or the fact that you care for him deeply. It's your mindset that changes everything. When you *need* him to text you back immediately, when you *need* to see him X amount of days per week, when you *need* him to be more affectionate, it's not enjoyable for him (or you!) and it feels like work. Your needs become a set of demands and requirements he has to fulfill. He has no choice, really; either he does what you want or he has to deal with you being upset or angry or annoyed.

It doesn't matter what you say or how you say it. What matters is the *intention* behind what you're saying. It either comes from a place of confidence and strength, or a place of insecurity and neediness. The words can be exactly the same, but the vibe will be totally different, and that makes all the difference.

## The Real Solution

*"Your task is not to seek for love, but merely to seek and find all the barriers within yourself that you have built against it."*

~ *Rumi*

You can't control another person; the more you try the more you'll fail. When you feel upset or resentful that he is taking the space he needs, or if he isn't meeting your expectations in some way, ask yourself why you want more of his time. Is it because you truly feel you don't spend enough time together and the relationship is suffering as a result? Are you feeling unfulfilled in your life and expect your partner to "fill you up" with something you are unable to give yourself? Are you jealous of the time he gives to others and think he ought to give more to you? Is it about him and the relationship, or are you putting your own needs first, at his expense? Take time to consider the real reason you feel you deserve more of his time and attention.

When you make requests of him that come from a need to control, and when you make him responsible for your feelings and well-being, you transmit a vibe that he will pick up on, and he will most likely react by feeling resentful, withdrawing from you, and resisting even further. This is when he'll feel like you're taking away his freedom, taking away his autonomy. And he will move further away in an unconscious attempt to get it back.

There is nothing wrong with wanting to spend quality time with your partner; in fact, it's essential to a healthy relationship. What matters is your *mindset*. If you genuinely believe the relationship is suffering, he will understand and will want to work with you to correct the problem. If you feel jealous or needy, then you need to work on resolving it within yourself, because he can't fix it for you. Reflect on what's going on inside of you, examine why you feel the way you do. What is the root source? What is the underlying fear?

I find that writing things out leads me to a place of clarity, so give that a try. Sometimes unpleasant feelings get stirred up and you may not instantly know where they're coming from. Before you blame him, write out what you're feeling and the possible reasons why you're feeling that way. When you hit the right one, you'll probably know it. Something will just click and it will send a *that's it* feeling of recognition throughout your body. If it's something within you, then try to work through it. You can also talk to him about it so he can better understand.

Sometimes we cling more tightly to a relationship and get upset over small things because we aren't feeling loved or cared for. The best way to approach this is to talk to him openly and honestly. Say something like "I appreciate you so much and know you are always trying to make me happy, but there are a few things I need in order to feel truly loved, and I will make it easier on you by telling you exactly what they are. If you can do this for me, we'll be all good. I need…" And tell him whatever it is. Personally speaking, I need a lot of quality time with my partner in order to feel loved and connected. If there are weeks where we don't get to spend much one-on-one quality time together, I notice myself becoming agitated and getting annoyed at him for small things. Once I realized the underlying reason behind this, I was able to communicate it clearly, and we worked together on resolving it.

When you communicate your feelings in an open and honest way, he doesn't feel trapped into doing certain things. He gains an awareness and understanding of what you need and then he happily gives it to you. When you tell him things in a way that still gives him a choice about how to act, you'll notice that he always chooses you.

## Let Him Choose You

*"Give the ones you love wings to fly, roots to come back to, and reasons to stay."*

*~ Dalai Lama*

A man's sense of freedom is bliss. Most men have to feel like they're empowered to make the decisions in their lives, or they will feel emasculated. If you take this away from them, they may even retreat or seem less at ease in your presence.

It's not that men don't want to commit, it's that men resent being backed into a corner and forced into something. It's not a matter of him not wanting to be official with you, or not wanting the relationship to progress, or not wanting to give you the love and affection you need, it's the feeling that he *has* to do something or you'll get upset. It all has to do with the way you broach the subject. Any woman who has experience with men has probably noticed that the more you push a man, the more he'll pull away.

When something is our choice, we don't feel locked into it. I have an arsenal of stories from my guy friends about girls who pressured them into being official, into saying I love you, into moving in together, into getting engaged. And all of those relationships ended.

Why? Because it wasn't a choice for the guy, it was an obligation; it became something he had to do or his girl would be upset. All people resent having their autonomy taken away, because it's a violation.

For example, I know a guy who was dating a girl for about seven months, and she was very much in love with him. He liked her and enjoyed the time they spent together… but he wasn't quite there yet. She told him she loved him first, and he didn't say it back. She understood at first. But then it kept coming up. Almost every time they hung out, she would ask him if he loved her, or she would tell him she loved him and give him a look like she was expecting him to say it back. It created an awkward and uncomfortable dynamic, but things trudged on.

During one particularly intense night, she managed to extract those three little words. He said them, but he didn't really mean them. It's not that he didn't think he would ever love her, and it's not that he didn't see a future with her. Sometimes it just takes longer with some people for these feelings to develop. She was placated by the fact that he'd finally said it, but it stirred up a lot of unpleasant feelings in him. He felt guilty because he didn't really mean it, and he felt pressured to catch up to her and fall in love. From that point on, love wasn't a choice, it was something he felt pressured into, and it completely blocked those feelings from naturally and genuinely developing. The relationship began to deteriorate and ultimately ended a few months later. I can't say for sure if he ever would have fallen in love with her naturally, given time, but I can confidently say that the pressure exerted on him to do so made it all but impossible.

The idea of letting a guy choose you gets twisted in modern dating advice. Women are told to hold back and play hard to get. But showing interest in a guy isn't the problem. Only a guy with extremely low self-esteem will run from a woman he likes when she really likes him. The problem is when he feels forced into something, or when he senses you have an agenda. A man can tell when you want him to do something out of a need for validation, as opposed to a genuine desire to deepen your connection with him, and it is off-putting.

When someone has an agenda, you don't enjoy being around that person and your guard reflexively goes up. Think about how you feel when someone is trying to sell you something. It doesn't matter how nice or friendly he seems; you know he has an agenda and you feel uneasy and proceed with caution.

The truth is, most men don't seek commitment. For the most part their mentality is, *I want to date around and I'll see what happens.* Commitment isn't so much the goal as it is a byproduct. It happens when a man finds a woman who enriches his life in a way he never could have on his own.

Wanting a commitment isn't an issue. And you don't need to hide the fact that this is what you want and play coy until he decides it's what he wants, too. The problem is when your need to love and be loved comes across as pressure. Fortunately, there is a way to communicate your needs in a way that invites him to commit rather than demanding it of him.

I know a guy in his forties who spent many years living it up as the archetypal bachelor. He wasn't opposed to commitment; it just wasn't something he was actively seeking. Then he met one woman who was different from the rest. Early into the relationship she said: "Is it in your playbook over the next few years to get married and stay married for the rest of your life? Because if it isn't, I want you to tell me now." He was surprised and impressed with her candor. He told me that had she said something along the lines of "I need a timeline for when we're going to get engaged" or "I need this to be exclusive or I'm leaving," he would have been out of there. The way she framed it didn't make him feel pressured, but she was still able to clearly communicate what she wanted, and what she would and wouldn't stand for. After a year of dating they got engaged and couldn't be happier.

Giving a man the freedom to choose applies not only to commitment, it extends to all aspects of a relationship. If you want him to do more nice things and be more romantic, you can express it to him without demanding it of him. When he feels like he *has* to see you or call you or text you, it will become a chore to him, another daily demand to add to his list of obligations. His choice in the matter is gone; either he does what you want or he has to put up with you getting on his case for not doing it. When you give a man the space to choose, he will usually move toward you. When you make demands or tell him what he *should* be doing, he will back away.

As we discussed in the previous chapter, the best way to encourage the "good behavior" you want while still allowing it to be his choice is to tell him what you want and to acknowledge and appreciate him when he does the things you like. And also, try not to take it personally when he doesn't or can't do exactly what you want. People get busy, life is unpredictable, and sometimes people just need time alone to recharge. In relationships the stakes are higher and our emotions are intensely involved, so we may blow these innocent things out of proportion.

It is also imperative to focus on keeping your mood positive and stable. The world of emotions can be scary and confusing and overwhelming at times, and often the things we get upset about are really no big deal. They become a big deal when you let them ruin your mood and send your mind spinning into a bad place. We can't control the things that happen to us, but we *can* control the way we react to them. Remember that, and try to find the power within you to take control of your mental and emotional state. Everything will change for the better once you do.

## Make This Your Mantra

- Freedom to a man is being able to do the things he needs in order to be his best self without fear that his girl will get upset or angry with him over it.
- Men often retreat when they are stressed out and overwhelmed, and prefer working through problems on their own rather than talking about it.
- When you interpret his need for space as him "not caring" or "not putting the relationship first," and try to force him to go back to the way he was before, you end up chasing a static, unrealistic version of the relationship and sucking the life out of it.
- Neediness is a mindset more than it is a set of behaviors. It doesn't come down to what you do or say, it's the intention behind your actions. When a woman is needy, she isn't receptive to what a man gives her because she is always desperate for more.
- When you give a man the space to choose, he will usually move toward you. When you make demands or tell him what he should be doing, he will back away.
- Men don't seek commitment and don't view it as a goal. A man commits quickly when he has the freedom to choose. A man resists commitment if he is backed into a corner.

## Exercise

- When you feel upset or resentful about something your guy is doing, like taking the space he needs to deal with a stressful situation, or if he isn't meeting your expectations in some other way, write down the behavior that is upsetting you. Now ask yourself why it is upsetting you. Don't analyze his behavior;

instead think about what your reaction say about you.

- Practice being okay. All the behaviors you engage in that he connects to having his freedom taken away — making requests of him that come from a need to control, making him responsible for your feelings and well-being — usually come from you not feeling okay. Notice when your mind sends you into alarm mode and tries to convince you there is a problem to solve, or that he doesn't love you. When you start to panic, and that voice within starts shouting that it's unacceptable that he did, or didn't do, X, realize that this is about you, not him. Silence the voice by saying "Everything is fine. I am okay." Take some deep breaths to connect back to your body and get to a more centered, balanced place.

## Resources

Check out the Chapter 6 resource section (www.anewmode.com/resource) for more content on why men pull away, how you should handle it, and more.

Articles include:

Ask a Guy: Why Do Men Withdraw?

The Top 3 Reasons Men Pull Away

A Guy's Take on Neediness

5 Common Misconceptions About Love

The Difference Between True Love and Unhealthy Obsession

Ask a Guy: Is He The One?

# Chapter 7: Men Live in the Moment

*"When you love someone, the best thing you can offer is your presence. How can you love if you are not there?"*

*~ Thich Nhat Hanh*

Do guys say what they mean? Yes... in the moment they say it, anyway. Personally speaking, I always had an impossible time trying to figure out how a man felt about me. I like words (I am a writer, after all!) and I take the things people say very literally. In my early dating years, I would find myself painfully confused time and time again by guys who would say really sweet things early on... only for everything to fizzle out.

I got so wound up because I was making the same mistake many women make — I was taking his words to be solid facts rather than expressions of fleeting feelings he was experiencing in the moment. Also like most women, I would jump way too many steps ahead any time I saw potential with a guy, and I would use any positive thing he said or did as proof that he wanted the same things I did. I didn't realize at the time that men don't experience relationships this way. In fact, I didn't have a clue about how men experience relationships. The main difference between men and women is that men typically don't have an end goal in mind that they're striving toward; they just take things as they come.

When you fixate on the outcome of a relationship, you are unable to enjoy the present moment and you choke the joy out of your own experience. The negative vibe you create coats your relationship and quickly poisons it, sometimes beyond repair. Instead of your guy feeling relaxed around you, he feels pressured (like he's afraid to offend you or upset you). Instead of you being his sanctuary and escape, you become a person (or vibe) that he wants to escape from.

Instead of him feeling like your presence fills him with joy and peace, he will feel like your presence drains him.

Men typically experience relationships in the moment, as they're unfolding. Women often jump several steps ahead and place expectations on the situation... sometimes they aren't even aware that this is what they're doing.

## When You Know the Truth...

When you understand how men experience relationships, you won't be confused about how he feels or where things are going. You won't analyze the things he says and does in an attempt to uncover hidden meanings. You'll accept his kind words and will continue to bring your best self to the relationship and will be able to comfortably allow the relationship to unfold organically.

When you understand what it is to live in the moment, you will free yourself from the endless cycle of high hopes followed by crushing disappointment. You will be able to navigate the relationship waters feeling at ease and calm, instead of being on alert, waiting for a tsunami to strike.

## Women Jump Ahead

I used to try to get to know the guys I dated in order to see if they matched my criteria for what I wanted in a man. Any piece of information he revealed would be met with a check or a minus. I think a lot of people unwittingly do this, approaching dates like they're interviewing job candidates. The thing to remember is that when you do this, you transmit a vibe that he will quickly pick up on. He can sense when he reveals something and you're disappointed by it (he doesn't like to travel, he doesn't play any instruments, he wants to leave the corporate world for a more meaningful job…whatever it is that earns him demerits in your mind), and it makes him more guarded and less sure of himself.

Think about going on a job interview. You can just tell the difference between an employer who is looking for reasons to hire you, for reasons why you are a good fit, and one who is looking for reasons not to, who is mentally tallying up all your flaws and the mistakes you made during the interview. In the first case you feel confident and at ease. You can be yourself and you feel good about it. In the second case, you feel uncomfortable and small. You feel stupid and insecure, like you can't get anything right.

I noticed that when I stopped sizing men up to see if they fit my standards, and instead went on dates with the intention of trying to get to know the person solely for the sake of getting to know him, I was never left wondering if a guy was going to ask me out again or how he felt about me. It was obvious to me that these men felt at ease and comfortable, and they always asked me out again.

If you want a guy to *not* ask you out again, just do the opposite. Spend the entire date judging him and reacting disapprovingly to certain personal disclosures, and he'll be done. Shameful confession: back in my former life as a serial dater, I would do this to guys I knew really liked me when I wasn't interested. I had such a hard time rejecting guys, and it seemed easier to create a situation in which they would reject me. And they would. I know it wasn't the most mature thing for me to do, but it just goes to show how significant your approval and appreciation are to him, and how obvious it is to him when you're jumping ahead, seeing him not simply for who he is, but what he can and can't do for you.

## Personal Story

Even though I knew better, I would slip up here and there when I started dating my husband and catch myself sizing him up. Any time I did this, especially times when I reacted negatively to something he disclosed, there would be an unmistakable shift in the vibe between us, and I would notice him becoming a little more reserved. Fortunately, I acted fast before I sabotaged things. Once I stopped analyzing, and instead made an effort to understand and appreciate him for exactly who he is, everything changed for the better and we were able to develop the kind of bond that inspires both of us to be our best selves. (Side note: When a man tells you that you bring out the best in him or that you make him want to be a better man, it pretty much means he's committed for life and you will have to do something catastrophic to change that.)

## Guy Confession

"I've dated girls in the past where I could tell they just wanted to hear certain things, or wanted me to be a certain way. In a lot of those cases I would end up hooking up with the girl but wouldn't pursue an actual relationship. I guess it becomes easier for me to objectify a girl if she isn't connecting to me as a real person. This is the main reason I'll decide not to continue dating a girl, because I don't feel like I can show her what I'm all about. It's not worth it for me because it will affect my self-esteem and how I regard myself if I put myself out there and she doesn't get me or understand who I am. A lot of guys aren't open right away, a girl needs to make the effort to pull it out of the guy. For me to be genuine, I need a girl to show genuine interest. If she doesn't, I won't even try to be genuine." - Kyle, 29

## Guys Don't Jump Ahead

A major difference between men and women I've noticed is in the way we approach and experience dating and relationships. Women usually seek commitment, and when they find a guy they think has the potential to give it to them, they tend to get swept up in thoughts and ideas for the future. They stop seeing what *is* and focus on *what could be.*

Men are not thinking about commitment or where the relationship is going. They are simply enjoying the time spent with you and building a bond and a connection. If it feels good, he'll keep going with it.

Men live in the moment. They are in the here and now, not in the five years from now. They don't analyze their emotions and they don't sit and ponder where things may be heading. They don't plan for a commitment; a commitment is just a natural development that occurs after a period of enjoying one another. The way men bond is similar to the way young children bond. Little kids bond though playing together... they don't make the bonding an end goal. Similarly, a man doesn't make bonding an end goal, it naturally happens when he spends time with a woman and both of them are able to be present, connected, and happy in each other's presence (as opposed to one of them trying to create a bond through some strategy, tactic, etc.)

What gets in the way of forming this type of connection is jumping ahead in your mind and creating what I call a "fantasy future." The problem with investing in a fantasy future is that it creates fear. You have a lot at stake in your mind and this naturally brings about a fear that things might not unfold the way you want. In other words, if that scenario plays out the way you want, you'll allow yourself to be happy. But if it doesn't, you erroneously believe that you will *lose something*... your life will become *less*... your life will *lack something*... you will no longer be *whole* or *complete*... you will somehow *lose a part of yourself.*

Your fantasy immediately sets up a "fear of loss," the loss of this future fantasy, so instead of enjoying every moment of your life, instead of allowing the relationship to unfold naturally, you do everything in your power to make this fantasy future come true. You throw away the joy of the present moment in favor of some fantasy future that will *make you* happy (as if happiness even worked that way). The reality is that you're just stressing yourself out and then *if* you get what you want, you will allow yourself some relief from the stress that *you created in the first place!*

## The Importance of Being Present

*"When we are liberated from our own fear, our presence automatically liberates others."*

~ *Nelson Mandela*

Your presence is the portal through which love can travel. If you're not present, that portal closes. The reason is simple: You can't connect to someone who isn't there... and you are where your thoughts are. If while you're with him you're constantly trying to figure out how he feels and where he stands and if there's a future... if you're constantly thinking about how amazing it will be to have him as a boyfriend... or husband... or father of your children... then you're not relating to him in the present moment. You're not there. When you're in analysis mode, you take yourself out of experience mode. And a relationship is an experience to be shared, not a thing you need to work to acquire.

It's subtler than you think. Being present means interacting with what is in that moment. If he texts you and you overthink how to respond and wonder: "How is this going to strike him? What will he think? Will this freak him out?" you are interacting with your own fears and the thoughts in your head. When he texts you and you write the response you feel without thinking, you're being present with him.

When a woman is happy and not looking to get a certain predetermined outcome from the relationship, she transmits an irresistible vibe that draws him in, and he naturally becomes more invested in her. There's a certain freedom to loving someone without needing or depending on that person for your happiness, and this freedom will cause him to want to commit to you on a deeper level.

The science behind it is pretty simple. If it feels good to be around you, he'll want to be around you more. When it becomes unpleasant, he'll want to be around you less. Men don't really look far beyond what's right in front of them.

The best way to be is to get your thoughts under control (especially when they are all fantasy-future-focused), don't rush things along, and try to live every day of the relationship like it's the first. Don't worry about where it's going — be present and just enjoy

I want to clarify that I am not saying you can't or shouldn't be excited... it *is* exciting when you start dating a new guy you click with. What I'm saying is don't get so attached to a certain outcome for the relationship that you don't allow the relationship to grow and unfold naturally. Sometimes we get so excited about the possibilities, we ignore red flags and signs of incompatibility that don't mesh with the outcome we want, and end up fighting to hang on to a fantasy future with someone who's not even right for us.

This doesn't just apply to the early phases of courtship. It's important to always try to be present with your man. Love and connection aren't ever givens. It's not like you cross some threshold and never have to think about them again. Your bond with your man needs to be fostered and nurtured, and this happens through your ability to be present.

I am also not saying you should never talk about the future or where things are going. These are conversations that are necessary at certain points, and there's nothing wrong with that. But let it happen naturally. When it happens naturally, you almost don't even feel the need to bring it up because you can feel that things are moving in a certain direction and you just know he's on the same page. That is what it is to flow in a relationship and let it unfold as it's meant to… and it is a glorious thing.

## Guy Confession

"I am always on guard when a girl goes all in too fast and I'd say most guys are. No guy wants to hurt a girl; it makes us feel like really terrible people. Girls get very attached quickly, every guy knows this, so if I'm not ready to handle it, and I'm not sure I want to go all in, I'll just end it. I went on three dates with this girl shortly after a really difficult breakup. I could tell she really liked me and that she was way more invested than I was. I did think she was a great girl, but I just wasn't ready to make the same level of investment in things as her so I ended it. She was devastated, but I think it would have been way worse if I'd let it drag on. Unless I know I want to go all in, I will cut out as soon as a girl gets too attached." - Marc, 33

## When a Guy Suddenly Loses Interest

The following scenario is something that came up more than a few times in my dating history: I'd meet a guy and feel that proverbial spark. Numbers would be exchanged, flirty texting would ensue, and then we would go on some really great dates. I would usually start out a little hesitant — a product of being burned so many times in the past — but the guy would come on full force and soon enough, I would give in to it… and I couldn't help but get excited about the possibilities. Is this finally it for me? Is he the one I've been waiting for? I could totally see myself with someone like him... he has everything I'm looking for! And then something would suddenly shift. He would become a little indifferent, a little less enraptured by me, slightly less engaged. It would be subtle, but still obvious enough to twist my stomach in knots and leave me constantly on edge... waiting for the next text... the next date... or maybe for the other shoe to drop...

Soon enough, he would either break up with me ("I just don't see it working out," aka the most vague breakup reason ever!) or completely ghost... never to be heard from again. It was incredibly frustrating, and my self-esteem took a real beating. What was I doing wrong? It must be *something!* And of course, this only seemed to happen with the guys I really liked, never with the ones I could take or leave. No, those guys would go all in, they would pursue me with everything they had. I knew I had those ones, even if they didn't text me for a few days, I knew they would... and they always did. And so I asked myself the same question that has been asked by many girls before and will be asked by many forevermore: Why is it I only get the guys I don't want, and never the ones I do?

This scenario is not unique to me. I hear about it from readers and see it happen to friends of mine all the time... and they are always left baffled by it. A big cause for this confusion is that when a girl loses interest in a guy after a few dates, she can usually pinpoint the reason. Maybe he was too desperate, not intellectually stimulating, too quiet, too loud, too boring, too boisterous — she usually knows exactly what it is that turned her off and can give a reason for why she doesn't want to continue dating him. It's usually not like this for guys. A guy can go on a few amazing dates with a girl and find himself suddenly and inexplicably put off by her. Even though he was previously texting her throughout the day and feeling a strong desire to see her... he now has no desire to contact her whatsoever. This can be as baffling for guys as it is for girls. When asked, many guys will say they don't know why they were suddenly turned off... they just were.

So why does this happen? Is it really out of the blue without cause or provocation? No, there is a reason. The reason it's so hard to pinpoint and articulate is because it's extremely subtle. But subtle doesn't mean lacking in power.

Here's how it usually goes down. On those first few dates, your vibe is typically pretty laid-back and easygoing. You want to explore the possibilities with this new guy and see what he's all about. It starts out light and fun; it's about connecting and enjoying each other's company. After a few great dates with a seemingly great guy, most women can't help but get excited about the possibilities. You are no longer in the here and now, seeing the situation for what it is. Instead, your mind is focusing on what it *could* be, and that's when it becomes a problem.

All anyone really wants is to feel okay, and most of us don't. When a woman worries and needs constant reassurance, it comes from a feeling of "I am not okay," and the underlying feeling is fear. What makes it so destructive is that it's not an overwhelming, gripping fear; it's a vague feeling of unease. It's so subdued and subtle you may not even realize it's there. You know how sometimes you'll be a little thirsty and go to take a sip of water, and you literally can't stop chugging? You didn't even realize you were so thirsty, it was only when you began to quench the initially faint thirst that you realized how potent it was. That's kind of what's at play here.

It can be tough for you to nail down the source of feeling not okay, but without even knowing what it is you will unconsciously latch onto things that you think will free you from this feeling, usually by seeking reassurance or trying to make situations come about that you feel will make you happy and finally grant you relief. This inevitably impacts your vibe and you become a parasite of sorts; everyone you come into contact with is simply a means to an end.

When you meet a guy who makes you feel okay, your need for that feeling becomes overwhelming and you latch on forcefully. You may not even realize you're doing it; it's not something you express outright. But it's there, and it comes across, even in the slightest ways. It changes your vibe and your energy, and guys feel this.

At this point, instead of him feeling like he's connecting with you, he feels like you're trying to get something out of him. Maybe it's reassurance or validation, or maybe just more of the feeling of being okay. Guys don't know exactly what it is, but suddenly their instincts are telling them to get away. This usually occurs at the point where the woman could no longer keep the act up. Maybe she's trying to appear cool and go with the flow, but in her mind she's already thinking of ways to turn a relationship that's really nothing at this point into something. From that point forward, it's not easygoing and natural; it's her measuring if she is getting closer to or further from her goal. Everyone recognizes when someone has an agenda; it's just something our intuition picks up on, and it immediately puts people off.

That's the switch that guys feel. It's the shift from things being easy and fun to agenda driven. When the woman feels like she's getting closer to her goal, she's happy and elated. When something happens that makes her feel like she is moving further away, she is gripped by that "my world is falling apart" feeling and may try to seek reassurance from the guy, either outright or subtly.

When you take a relationship that is brand new and start thinking that it's something, or try forcing it to be more than it is, it's game over. Your vibe will become man-repelling and before long, he'll be gone and you will be left baffled, analyzing what exactly you did to drive him away. But you won't ever find the answer, because it isn't concrete and measureable.

If you just enjoy life and engaging with him and don't try to make something out of it, your vibe will still be enjoyable and he will want to continue seeing you. When he feels good around you, he'll want to be around you. When he feels like you're trying to get something out of him, he will want nothing to do with you.

## Eric Confession

"I'll admit that I have gone from being super interested in a girl to being totally put off. When it happens, it's usually because the girl transforms and suddenly, instead of the situation being light, easy, and fun, I feel this pressure that if I don't do something or say something or be some certain way, she'll be unhappy and will passive-aggressively punish me for it. The girl will loop me into her sense of emotional well-being. At first, she showed up shiny and happy, and now she is someone who is trying to extract the shine and happiness from me. It's not something she's bringing to the table, it's something she is trying to extract, and it's extremely off-putting.

I started seeing this girl a while back and things were great at the beginning. I really enjoyed her company and looked forward to the times I could spend with her. My life is so stressful and busy most of the time, and she gave me relief from that... and it felt really nice. After a few weeks of hanging out, we slept together... and then things took a very sharp turn. Now she was no longer happy and light. She would get mad at me for not texting enough, for not taking her on enough romantic dates, for looking in another girl's direction. It was obvious that she was trying to turn this into something, and she was getting angry at me for not complying with her agenda.

I liked things how they were, and maybe it could have eventually evolved into something more meaningful, but once she had an agenda, I just felt too much pressure and completely lost interest in continuing the relationship."

## Don't Measure the Milestones

*"The love you feel in life is a reflection of the love you feel in yourself."*

*~ Deepak Chopra*

Men don't sit around plotting and wondering when the relationship will hit its next milestone... they just go with it and let it unfold, knowing things will move forward when it feels right and not by force.

At the same time, there are definitely guys who have an agenda or try to force a relationship in a certain direction. If you've ever experienced it, I'm sure you found it off-putting, and maybe even a little creepy. I dated a guy like that once. He was cute and charming and successful, but after only two weeks of dating he wanted to be official and wouldn't let it go when I said I needed more time. I had gone through a horrific breakup the year before and my ability to trust and commit wasn't yet fully repaired. Even though I explained this to him, he wouldn't ease up. Soon enough every conversation centered on us being official... and why I didn't want to go there just yet. I wasn't flattered by his eagerness — I was concerned by his desperation. I mean, why did this guy want a girlfriend so badly? Was he bad with women? Was he so insecure that he needed a label? I was immediately put off by his persistence, and the relationship didn't last much longer.

The reason people, both guys and girls, get hung up on the label or hitting some milestone is because they use it as a measure of their self-worth. The thing is... it will never give you that. Relationship milestones will not make you feel loved or secure if you don't already feel loved and secure. Instead, you will be like a junkie on a constant quest for the next high… the high being validation.

Maybe it starts with you thinking: *As soon as he calls me his girlfriend, I'll feel secure.* Then if he does, you think: *As soon as he says 'I love you' I'll feel secure…* if he does, you anxiously wait for him to say it again. If he doesn't say it for a few days you wonder: Does he not love me anymore? The next mark is moving in together, or maybe getting engaged. So you get engaged, or move in, and you feel relieved temporarily, but it doesn't last.

There are going to be days when he isn't 100% loving and affectionate. And on those days, you'll wonder if he's having doubts, if he changed his mind, if he's losing interest. The cycle literally will never end. The only way to stop it is to focus on genuinely loving yourself and believing the people you love will love you back.

If you don't genuinely love yourself, you will never fully trust that anyone else can love you. Period. It doesn't matter what he says or does. He can be the most loving, over the top, romantic guy on the planet, and it will never ever truly sink in. It will feel like relief at least for a moment, but it won't last. The reason it won't penetrate is because you can only let in as much love from the outside as you feel for yourself on the inside.

A lot of women miss this entirely, so they seek a man to give them this fulfillment. Doing this actually hinders their chances of finding true love, but if they do happen to land in a relationship, they won't really be able to enjoy it. They won't fully trust it. They may pin this sense of insecurity on the guy and blame him for not making them feel loved. If only he did this, then I'd feel okay. If only he told me he loved me more often… if only he called just to say hi… if only he were more affectionate… if only he were more romantic… if only he complimented me more.

120

Even if the guy does say I love you every hour, even if he does call and text constantly, even if he showers her with compliments, she'll always find something else he *could* be doing to make her feel loved. What happens then is the guy feels like nothing he does is enough and he simply can't make her happy. So he either leaves or becomes filled with resentment, which only worsens the underlying problem.

The point is, you must put your focus on self-love rather than romantic love. Being in a loving relationship can be enormously beneficial and transformative. It can increase your happiness, it can help you grow and become a better person, it can make you feel truly loved and cared for, but *only if* you already love yourself and are working on ways to become your best self on your own, completely outside of the relationship. It isn't easy, and for some it can be downright brutal. But it is essential.

## How I Got There

*"Nothing ever goes away until it teaches us what we need to know."*

~ *Pema Chodron*

I had a lot of old wounds from childhood and early adulthood that were seriously blocking me from letting anyone in. I felt repulsed by guys who genuinely cared about me, and drawn to what I refer to as the "damage cases" — the guys who were emotionally unavailable, had issues to work out, who couldn't commit, or who just couldn't reciprocate my feelings. Maybe it just felt safer and more familiar somehow. It was also validating in a sad way. I subconsciously believed I wasn't worthy of love and was drawn to men who couldn't truly love me, thus validating my sad belief. That's the thing about the subconscious mind… it will always seek ways to validate long-held beliefs, even if they don't serve us and actually harm us.

I knew this had been my pattern for quite some time, but I think I kind of assumed it would sort itself out over time. It didn't. I kept finding myself in the same situations over and over again. After learning the same lesson for maybe the hundredth time, I realized that something needed to change; I couldn't keep doing the exact same thing and expecting different results.

I wish it were as easy as having an epiphany and suddenly everything snapping perfectly into place. I thought that's what would happen, but core beliefs that have been created and built up over time don't just evaporate in a moment. In time, I realized I really needed to work through some issues. I started seeing an amazing therapist, journaling, reading books on topics related to issues I was having, opening up more to close friends and nurturing those relationships (there is an enormous healing power in being your authentic self and feeling safe doing so).

It took some time, but eventually my faulty wiring was corrected and I came to a place of genuine self-love and self-respect. As they say, old habits die hard, and so I did slip up here and there and get sucked in by the "damage cases," but eventually guys like that became completely unappealing to me. In fact, I felt a little sorry for them. I hoped they would work through whatever issues they had, but there was no part of me that wanted to be the one to nurse them back to psychological health.

I committed myself to getting to the root of my damage case addiction, and after a few months of posing the tough questions of myself and answering them... an old flame from high school popped back into my life, and we've been together ever since. I knew I had successfully healed from those old wounds because he was emotionally available, he was loving, he was committed, he was crazy about me... and this didn't turn me off, it actually made me love him more.

# Make This Your Mantra

- Men don't have an end goal in mind when they begin a relationship. They don't have a vision of where it will lead, and instead experience it in the moment, as it's unfolding.
- When a woman jumps ahead and invests in a fantasy future, she becomes filled with fear and is no longer able to be present and in the moment. This blocks a true connection from forming.
- Your presence is the portal through which love can travel. Being present means interacting with what is in the moment, and not with the thoughts and fears in your mind.
- When a woman is happy and not looking to get validation from the relationship, she transmits an irresistible vibe that draws her guy in, and he naturally becomes more invested in her and the relationship.
- Guys can intuit when you have a goal or agenda, and it is immediately off-putting. This is usually the reason why a guy suddenly loses interest completely, even if things were going great up until that point.
- You will never be satisfied in your relationship unless you learn to truly love yourself. If you don't genuinely love yourself, you will never fully trust that anyone else can love you.

# Exercise

Relationships, even the toxic ones, can lead to enormous growth if we look deep within ourselves and properly reflect on them. If done right, this can open the gates to allow the right person to walk through. What helped me was looking back at my toxic relationships and asking myself the following questions.

1. Grab a pen and paper, pick a toxic relationship, and write down the answers to these questions:

- Why was I drawn to him?

- What need did he fulfill for me?
- What did I like about him?
- Why did I stay even though he didn't treat me the way I wanted to be treated?
- What did I do in this relationship that I won't do again in the next?
- What did I learn from this relationship that I can use in a healthy way in my next relationship?

2. Focus on being present and in the moment. Try to engage with what's happening in the here and now, instead of interacting with the thoughts and worries in your mind.

When you catch yourself jumping ahead in your mind to a fantasy future, or analyzing your guy's behavior, stop and write down what you were thinking, then write down what you missed in the moment while you were stuck in your head.

## Resources

Visit the resource section for Chapter 7 (www.anewmode.com/resource) to learn more about common relationship pitfalls and steps you can take to have a relationship that is fun and enjoyable, not one filled with stress and worry.

Articles include:

Ask a Guy: How Do I Get Him to Commit?

How to Stop Stressing When It Comes to Dating and Relationships

5 Ways to Ruin a Budding Relationship

Why Guys Disappear and How to Deal

The Number One Reason Men Suddenly Lose Interest

How to Have a Healthy Relationship

# Chapter 8: Men Communicate Through Actions More Than Words

*"Part of the reason that men seem so much less loving than women is that men's behavior is measured with a feminine ruler."*

~ *Francesca M Cancian*

Eric and I wrote an e-book called *He's Not That Complicated* (www.anewmode.com/hntc). When I tell the title to guys, they nod in agreement and usually say: "Yup, so true. Men are simple." When I share the title with girls they cry: "What do you mean? Men are *so* complicated!" No, they really aren't. But if you've ever felt that way, then this is the chapter you need to pay the most attention to.

A major reason we girls get confused by men, and spend so much time trying to figure out how a guy feels, is because we wait to hear the words and overlook the fact that men say a lot more through their actions. What a man says is oftentimes not an accurate measure of how he feels, while his actions nearly always tell the real story.

## When You Know the Truth

Communication is the key to any successful relationship, so when you can truly understand how men communicate you will open the door to a stronger connection. Most fights occur because one person isn't feeling loved or cared for, but instead of saying this outright (and sometimes not even realizing that's what's going on), a girl might start a fight about something stupid. Let's say a guy had a really busy day and took a few hours to text his girl back. She knows on one level that this really isn't a big deal, and she knows that his days can get hectic. But if she's already starting to question how he feels, or she isn't feeling particularly loved, then this "no big deal" can turn into a major fight.

One major reason women don't always feel loved, or know how a guy feels, is because there are innate communication differences between men and women. Women cling to words. Men, however, simply aren't as verbal and can't always articulate what they're feeling as well. Often a woman can get so caught up in waiting to hear certain words, that she completely overlooks all his loving actions.

## Men Are Less Verbal

Countless studies have demonstrated that men simply don't use as many words in a day as women do. And when men do speak, they don't usually speak about their emotions, they speak as a means to achieve something, like making a plan.

Men don't form connections through talking. A man can bond with another man by just sitting in silence watching the game. If two women were sitting together in silence you would think they were mad at each other!

While women are the ones deemed "emotional," both genders have the same capacity to experience emotions… the difference is that men have been conditioned by society not to show their emotions. They grow up being told to man up, that boys don't cry, that being vulnerable is a sign of weakness. As a result, men aren't as expressive and forthcoming with their emotions, and saying everything he thinks and feels doesn't come naturally to him.

Think about the way boys form friendships in their developmental years as opposed to girls. Boys typically bond through activities. If they both like basketball or root for the same team or love video games, they become friends and they get together and do those activities. Girls also form friendships based on shared interests, but it goes deeper even at early ages. Girls will stay up late and share their feelings, what makes them happy and sad, their hopes and dreams and fears. This is not what goes on at the boy slumber parties.

Boys really only enter the realm of emotional disclosure when they get older and start forming friendships and relationships with girls. This isn't to say that men emerge from adolescence emotionally stunted, but a lot of them do have trouble tapping into their emotions and sharing them.

Getting frustrated with him about this won't get you anywhere, it will just make him less inclined to open up. Whenever a woman is displeased with her guy he intuitively picks up on it and he feels like he's a loser because he's disappointing her. When he feels safe and accepted for who he is, that's when he will start to share.

## Men Measure Relationships by How They Feel with You

When it comes to relationships, guys don't get caught up in how frequently a girl texts or what she says. Guys look at how well you connect with who he is. He looks to see if you get him, if you appreciate him, if you accept him. He'll look to see if you laugh at his jokes, if you understand his humor, if you understand his personality and don't expect or want him to be some other way. And most importantly, he looks at how enjoyable the time he spends with you is. Does he feel free to be himself, or does he have to create a persona and put on some sort of act to win you over?

A persona can be charming and enticing, but it isn't real. It is a result of having your guard up. Your personality emerges when your guard is down and you can just be who you are and see if you can connect with the other person in a real way. If you are both interacting in an authentic, unguarded way and it's a match, it will feel good, it will make sense, and you will feel a deep connection.

A man measures a relationship by how much of a flow exists between the two of you and how free he can be with you. He might not be the best verbal communicator, so you'll miss it if you get hung up on his words.

After the courtship and infatuation phases pass and you both commit... after you hit all the milestones... you're in love, you get engaged, you get married... then there is just spending time together. You need to be comfortable with that person. You need to be able to just *be*, to not feel like you have to put energy into aligning with the other person. Maybe this is challenging and exciting at first, but it gets exhausting over time and you just can't keep up the ruse forever.

At the end of the day, we all want someone who accepts us as we are and who just fits with us seamlessly, no force necessary.

## Personal Story

I dated a guy years ago I really liked. He said a lot of things that indicated he really liked me too, but I couldn't quite tell where he really stood. We were hanging out a day after he got back from a trip to Aruba with his family (a yearly tradition), and after telling me about the trip he said: "Maybe next year you'll come too." I took this to be a major relationship milestone — he *obviously* saw a future with me or why would he bring up me going on vacation with his family?! Never mind the fact that we weren't an official couple, that he didn't send me a single text or e-mail for the entire ten days he was gone, that he didn't really prioritize spending time with me... I didn't factor in any of that.

He also mentioned something about us going to a Jay-Z concert that summer (it was winter), and I took it to mean he saw a future and intended to be with me that long. Interestingly enough, it was right around this point that his interest in me started to wane. We had been seeing each other for maybe two months, a point at which the relationship should have been moving along, but instead we seemed to be going backward. I heard from him less often, we didn't spend much time together, and he would disappear for days at a time. Eventually he faded away completely. My confusion over this had many sources (all of which I discuss in great depth in the introduction to *He's Not That Complicated*), but the main area where I got stuck was why he would say all those sweet things and make plans for the future when he wasn't serious!

I spoke to my male roommate and some of his guy friends about the issue and they all laughed at me for thinking the words meant something. They told me that guys sometimes say things in the moment because it feels good in the moment. Regarding the vacation, he was probably thinking, "This girl is really cool. Yeah, she should totally come on the vacation, that would be awesome!" and that was it. He wasn't thinking of the implications or the future or me actually meeting his family. It was just a thought that popped into his head in the moment and nothing more. I stayed in the relationship for way longer than I should have, clinging to the things he said as pillars of hope, when really his actions said it all.

## Focus on What He Does, Not on What He Says

*"When someone shows you who they are believe them; the first time."*

~ *Maya Angelou*

What a man says is oftentimes the worst indication of how he feels... unless his actions sync up with what he's saying.

It's not that men are intentionally trying to trick you or delude you. Men are very in the moment, as discussed in the previous chapter, and they don't always weigh their words as carefully as women do.

Words, in general, don't mean as much to men as they do to women. Men are much more action oriented while women typically prefer to express themselves verbally. Men experience relationships as they're unfolding, without leaping miles ahead and wondering where things are going and if there's a future. Oftentimes, at a given moment a guy could be thinking, "Wow, this is a great girl, I really like her and am enjoying being with her," and he might express this. While the girl might take this to mean that he sees a future and is serious about her, he may not even be close to that point.

This doesn't mean you should never take what he says seriously; if his actions sync up with his words, then he means it. And if a man is serious about the relationship, he won't say things unless he really means them.

When a man isn't serious, you're dealing with a whole different animal. For instance, if he's a guy you hook up with sometimes and he texts you things like he's crazy about you, he likes you, you're the coolest girl he's ever met... but he doesn't ask you out, he just summons you over when he's horny, then maybe he thinks you're fun, but if he were serious about you he would take it beyond casual hookups. A lot of us make the mistake of holding onto the words... thinking that someday his actions will align. It doesn't work like that. He will usually show you through his actions that he cares and the words will come after.

For those who like things presented in more concrete terms, here it is. If a guy tells you he really likes you and you are the most amazing woman he has ever known and introduces you to his friends and family, factors you into his decisions, is there for you when you need him, tries to make you feel special, and is affectionate, then by all means, believe him!

If a guy tells you those exact same words but doesn't want to be official, keeps you totally separate from everyone else in his life, disappears for days at a time, cancels plans at the last minute, asks you to come over in the middle of the night, hooks up with other girls, won't make your relationship public in any way, keeps checking online dating accounts... well then please, don't believe him and instead run far and fast.

## Getting Him to Open up

Men don't open up as easily as women about their feelings. As I said, it just doesn't come as naturally for them. This can be incredibly frustrating for us... *We just want to know what he's thinking and feeling... why won't he just tell us?!* It's not that he's holding out on you, or he doesn't want to let you in; sometimes he just doesn't have the language to articulate whatever is going on in his heart and mind.

Most men feel misunderstood and have been brought up to believe that talking about emotions makes them wimps. Sharing his feelings isn't always comfortable or easy for him, and he has a lot of fears attached to putting himself out there like that. Try to remember that this may be relatively new to him and don't push too hard for him to open up. All you need to do is be patient and when he does reveal things to you, listen to him without judgment. Show him that it's okay for him to talk honestly about his feelings and more than that, it actually makes you love and appreciate him more. The more he feels safe sharing with you, the more comfortable he will become.

If he doesn't want to share, then try to be okay with that, too, and respect his wishes. And don't withhold and stop sharing your feelings until he does. Think of yourself as his tour guide into the realm of emotional disclosure by showing him how to talk about feelings; the best way may be to tell him how you're feeling.

A lot of us get so caught up in our own needs, our own wants, or own insecurities that we forget that our man has needs, insecurities, and wants of his own. We fixate on our own story and forget to say, "I'm sorry you had such a rough day," or "Wow I can't believe you stood up to your boss like that, I know it must have been tough, but it must have felt great!" A man isn't always going to come out and tell you what he wants and needs from you. Fortunately, we women have the gift of intuition and can pick up on these things when we can get out of our own heads. Try to pay attention to some of his unspoken needs and nurture them. Doing this will strengthen your emotional connection and will make communicating about emotional things easier for him.

Again, it all comes from you being in a good place emotionally. It comes from you loving yourself and not needing him to validate you. When you are in this place, you want him to open up because you want your connection to grow, you want to understand him, you want him to understand you. When you aren't in this place, you want to know what he's thinking and feeling because these things have implications for your own sense of well-being and for your fantasy future. If he seems upset about something, your concern comes more from your worry that you did something wrong, that he's not happy with you, that it will impact your plans for the outcome of the relationship, rather than a genuine concern for him and what's going on in his world right now.

If you need a bit more verbal affirmation from him, tell him how much it means to you when he says what he loves about you. Tell him how safe, how secure, how warm and good it makes you feel. Whatever it is you want to hear, tell him why it's important to you and how good it makes you feel. As you know, a man wants to

132

make you happy so when you tell him what you want in a kind, loving way, he will make an effort to do it.

## Guy Confession

"I have a hard time opening up verbally and I think most guys do. When I first started dating my girlfriend, she would always complain that she wanted me to share more and to let her into my inner world. I really tried, but it just didn't come naturally to me. I was resistant at first because it seemed like she was just trying to get assurance from me, like she didn't trust me. I loved spending time with her and introduced her to my family and friends, I thought it was obvious that I was super into her, but she kept pushing for more and it just stressed me out. Eventually she eased up and over time, I was naturally able to share my feelings verbally. It's always a bit of a struggle, but I try my best because I know it's important to her." - Alex, 30

## Men and Texting

We can't talk about communication without discussing the number one mode of communication these days: texting! Eric and I get absolutely flooded with questions from readers who are completely confused by their guy's texting habits. He doesn't text back, he doesn't initiate texting, he stops texting in the middle of a conversation. The sad fact is, men have absolutely *no* idea how intensely their texting habits are being scrutinized. *None!*

Men don't place the same significance on certain things as women do. While women see constant texts as a sign that a guy really likes them, men don't see text messages and two-hour-long phone calls as necessary or important for bonding and building relationships.

To him, using his phone is just a means to an end. It's a way to quickly coordinate plans and get things done. It's not the important interpersonal tool that it is for a lot of women. Sometimes a man will stop responding because he doesn't see the point in talking unless it's for the sake of making a plan. Or sometimes he'll just run out of things to say because it's just not natural for him to talk and talk (or rather, text and text), just for the sake of talking or texting.

When a man doesn't return a text or a call immediately, it is not an accurate indicator of disinterest. He's most likely busy or focused on something else at the moment.

Guys evaluate the quality of their relationship by the quality of the time spent with the other person. You can't measure the depth of a relationship by the number of texts received on average per day, or by how much time elapses between each text. You measure the depth of a relationship by the *quality* of the time you spend with the other person. You can spend all day texting back and forth with some guy about nonsense. This doesn't mean you have a great and profound relationship, it doesn't really mean... anything.

Another important difference between men and women is that most men aren't as good at multitasking. Men simply have a tougher time switching gears and turning their attention to something else once they are fully absorbed in a project. This makes sense from an evolutionary standpoint because once upon a time, a man had to go out and hunt in order to feed his family. To do this, he had to focus his attention 100% on the task at hand; a moment of being distracted or trying to deal with something else could lead to him being attacked by a wild beast! Even though these days we get meat from the supermarket, a man's brain is fixed and focused, and he just can't juggle several tasks all at once.

A woman can be at work doing her job and also G-chatting all day with a guy she likes. She can manage to do a great job at work while simultaneously focusing on her relationship. Men usually can't operate like this. A guy will have a much tougher time "being in" the relationship when he's at work. When he's at work, that is his focus and there is no other reality. How this manifests is a guy not texting a girl back when he's at work, or being short and dismissive if he speaks to her during the workday.

When you send him text after text and each time his phone dings and he has to pick it up, his attention is diverted from whatever it was he was focusing on. If he gets distracted enough times, he'll put his phone on silent and completely ignore it until he finishes whatever he's working on. Meanwhile, you are on the other end getting frustrated and wondering why he stopped texting and what it means. You may ask him later why he stopped responding. If he says he was busy, you might say that's no excuse — he could have taken *five seconds* to send you a reply. But the reality is, although it may seem easy enough in your mind, it isn't that simple for him. He simply isn't able to ping pong his attention back and forth with the same ease as you.

Some women get confused because in the beginning of a relationship, a guy may be more inclined to text back and forth all day. However, this isn't sustainable. If he wants to keep his job, he won't be able to produce the same high volume of texts per day as he did in the beginning. As I mentioned, men are goal-oriented and usually communicate as a means to an end. In the beginning, he prioritizes constant communication because he is trying to win you over and wants to establish himself as a presence in your life. Once you settle into a relationship, he no longer sees a need to engage in this sort of thing and he stops. Women take this to mean he is losing interest, but really it just means that things have become more established and comfortable... and that's a good sign!

When a man doesn't return a text or a call immediately, it is not an accurate indicator of disinterest. He's most likely busy or focused on something else at the moment, so there is zero need to stress over it.

## Guy Confessions

"Girls expect a response even to texts that don't require a response. For instance, "I'm going to watch a movie tonight" is not a text that *needs* a response. A better text is, "What movie should I watch?" If the guy doesn't respond then he's probably busy. If it's a pattern of behavior for him to always ignore your texts, then he doesn't like you very much. Leave him." - Nate, 26

"Guys don't like to be bothered during the day. We have one-track minds and lose focus easily. Personally, I keep my phone on silent during the day so I don't see texts immediately. I have things I want to get done, and every text with a girl is a distraction. It's nothing personal, it's just how we operate. I'm seeing a girl right now and she will sometimes text me during the day to say hi or that she's thinking about me, and it feels really nice and can actually light up my day. On the other hand, I have dated girls who would constantly text me and demand a response, or get upset if I didn't reply right away, and this was very draining and I didn't stay in those relationships for very long. A guy can tell if a woman is reaching out just because she wants to, or if she's reaching out because she's insecure and needs attention or reassurance from him." - Brad, 29

## Make This Your Mantra

- Don't measure how a man feels by what he says. Look at what he does.
- Men don't bond through talking, they bond through shared experiences. Guys don't measure the quality of a relationship by what is said, they measure it by how they feel with the girl.
- It's not that men don't want to express themselves verbally, it just doesn't come as easily to them as it does to women, due to their gender and societal conditioning. Sometimes he simply doesn't have the language to articulate how he's feeling.
- A man measures a relationship by how much of a flow exists between the two of you and how free he can be with you. He might not be the best verbal communicator, so you'll miss it if you get hung up on his words.
- You can trust that his feelings are true if his actions sync up with his words. If he doesn't show you he cares through his actions, it means he doesn't.
- When a guy doesn't text back, it's usually for an innocent reason (he was busy or he didn't think the last text called for a response). When you can't accept this, you turn a non-issue into a problem.
- Men measure the quality of a relationship by the quality of the time spent with the other person, not by the quantity of texts sent per day.

## Exercise

Practice looking at the ways your guy shows you he loves you through his actions. Maybe he did the dishes after you cooked. Maybe he gave you a massage after a long day, or took you to your favorite restaurant, or went to a family function with you even though a big game was on. Maybe it's the way he looks at you, the way he hugs you, the way he speaks to you. Try to zero in on how he communicates "I love you" without actually saying it.

At the end of each day for one week, write down at least one loving action your guy took that day. Or keep a running list throughout the day on your phone or somewhere handy. Whenever you start to become unsure of his feelings for you because he's not being verbal enough about it, refer to this list.

## Resources

Learn more about how men communicate, and how you can effectively reach your man, in the resource section for Chapter 8 (www.anewmode.com/resource).

Articles include:

How to Solve Issues Without Ruining Your Relationship

Ask a Guy: Does My Boyfriend Really Mean What He Says?

Ask a Guy: Why Does He Take So Long to Text Back?

The Real Reasons It Drives You Crazy When He Doesn't Text Back

# Chapter 9: If You Give a Guy What Makes Him Want to Commit, He Will Commit

*"You cannot make someone love you. You can only make yourself someone who can be loved."*

*~ Derek Gamba*

Whether it's having the official "girlfriend" title, being official on Facebook, getting a guy to move in together, getting him to propose, or reigniting a flickering spark, there are countless women all over the world struggling to get the commitment they want from their man. (Even married women struggle with this!) And it's a sucky feeling.

I've been there. I once dated a guy for six months who wouldn't acknowledge me as his official girlfriend. This sort of thing can have a devastating effect on your self-esteem, as you essentially wind up living your life on some quest to prove that you're worthy of his commitment. You may alternate between being overly accommodating and sweet (to show him how easygoing and amazing you are and what a great girlfriend/domestic partner/wife you'll be) or getting mad and lashing out at him for everything, even though you're really only mad at him for *one* thing.

Sometimes you'll feel compassionate and will convince yourself that as soon as he's more established at his job... as soon as he gets over his baggage... as soon as he is less stressed out... as soon as we stop arguing so much... *then* he'll take the next step. Other times you'll get angry and think *I don't deserve this* and fights will ensue... but you won't leave, because you've already come so far!

# When You Know the Truth...

You will realize that getting a man to commit isn't like playing a game of chess. You don't need to master an intricate set of rules and utilize a strategy. It's not about tricking him or trapping him. Despite what you have heard, men are not anti-relationship, men are not commitment-phobes, and men actually do want to find that one special someone to share their lives with. Getting a man to commit isn't all that complicated, it really comes down to whether you create an environment that makes him want to commit... or you don't.

It's not a matter of you being worthy or unworthy, of him being commitment-phobic or not, all that matters is how you make him feel and what you add to his life. Do you make his life a better place or a more stressful place? Are you his retreat or something he needs to retreat from?

When you know what it takes, then you can allow the relationship to unfold organically without any worry or stress. And you will realize that if it takes an incredible amount of effort and doesn't seamlessly come together, it means it isn't the right relationship, and you will move on with your sense of self firmly intact.

## Are You Making His Life a Better Place?

Men don't believe they will *get* anything from a relationship. They don't believe it will complete them or make them happy in the way a lot of women do.

Commitment for a man comes down to this: Is my life better with her in it or not? If the answer is yes, he commits.

Men don't go out seeking commitment; their drive is to date around. But if a man is with a woman and whenever he's with her, he simply feels better than when she's not there, then he'll want to keep her around and will want the relationship to last. When he's been with her so long that he can't imagine life without her and sees "commitment" as something that's already established anyway, he'll be "officially" committed.

Most guys feel pretty beat up and battered on a daily basis. To have a sanctuary from the cruel realities of life and to have a place of true safety, comfort, and understanding can be pretty irresistible. The right relationship can bring more happiness, fun, and inspiration to his life than he even knew could exist. It creates a feeling inside him that says, "I am going to win in life with this woman by my side."

I want to again emphasize that it has to be the *right* relationship. The thing to always remember is not everyone is a great fit for each other. Yes, there are plenty of relationship skills you can learn and develop to create more harmony in your relationship and help you and your partner communicate more effectively, but even still, some people just don't work as a couple.

Usually problems arise when a woman doesn't feel loved and a man doesn't feel appreciated, and neither one knows how to give the other person what they need, because it's just not in their nature to be that way. I have a friend who was in one of those relationships where if they could go two straight days without fighting it was something of a miracle. The biggest issue was she wanted her boyfriend to be more mushy and affectionate and soft, and that just wasn't how he was wired. He would try to be sweeter, to pay her more compliments, but no matter what he did, he couldn't get to the level of "mush" she wanted. He felt unappreciated and defeated, and she felt unloved and frustrated.

When a guy's personality isn't exactly what you want, you can guide him by telling him certain things he can do to make you feel

141

loved, but you also need to accept that you can't change him as a person. Some people are very emotional, some are more intellectual. Some people are soft and sensitive, some are straightforward and direct. Some people are outgoing and others are more reserved. If you fight against what someone's nature is, you will always lose.

Sometimes incompatibility is a matter of two people just having wildly different ways of processing the world and their emotions and not being able to find common ground. Again, the choice you have to make is whether you can accept him the way he is or not. If it bothers you and always will, then it will probably end up being the root cause of the majority of your fights. The point I'm trying to hammer in is that sometimes it just isn't a match. This has nothing to do with your worthiness, attractiveness, or who you are as a person. You don't become best friends with every person you meet — there are people you instantly click with and get along with and people who just aren't your cup of tea. A relationship is much more intense than a friendship, even a best friendship, and no amount of skills or tactics can change lackluster levels of chemistry and compatibility.

Now, back to making his life a better place. When you are in a good place yourself internally, and you and he are compatible and have a high level of chemistry, then he will feel strong and inspired in your presence. You won't have to *do* anything, you can just be who you are. Of course it will take time to know specific things about him, to know exactly how he operates and what he needs at certain times and how to give it to him, but even still, it will come pretty easily. And you will find the discovery process fun and exciting, not stressful, confusing, or emotionally draining.

# It's Not About the Chase

The men who end up committing intensely are the ones who see the woman as their partner, the woman who "gets" them, the woman who's on their side, the woman they escape to, the woman they love being around, the woman who lights up their world…

This doesn't happen if he feels like he doesn't have her. That "chasing" dynamic requires her to keep up her guard and objectifies every interaction in the relationship. It also *kills* any chance for true love to develop.

Girls think that playing hard to get will make a guy like them, and being too available will turn him off. This isn't true. Waiting a certain amount of time before texting him back and pretending to be busy when you're not doesn't get a guy to like you, it gets a guy to chase you. Does it work? Maybe a little, in that it activates his competitive drive, but that isn't the recipe for lasting love. You can't manipulate someone into feeling something for you… I mean you can, but your true self will emerge eventually… and then what?

In situations where you felt you were chasing a guy, you might have desperately wanted him, but did you feel like you could *trust* him? *Depend* on him? Did you feel *loved*?

The problem with the chase is that it creates the illusion of having chemistry. Whoever is doing the chasing never knows what to expect, and it stirs up feelings inside that can be mistaken for an intense desire to be with the other person, when really it's just a desire to get validation by making the other person want to be with you.

I have a friend who always winds up in relationships with guys who won't commit to her in a real way. She has let a few of these situations drag on for years! Every one of the guys would manage to keep her on the hook by telling her he loved her, he cared about her, he really wished he could commit to her... but he just couldn't for whatever reason. After finally cutting it off with yet another guy who strung her along for over a year, she started dating a guy who was different from the rest. He liked her a lot (and it was obvious!), he expressed a desire to have a committed relationship, he asked to be exclusive after almost a month, he introduced her to his mom soon after. It was a drama-free, effortless, easy relationship.

The catch? She came to me and said "I just don't feel the same chemistry with him as I did with the other guys!" When we talked it out, it became clear that the "chemistry" she thought she had with the others was really just her not fully having them. In those "chase" relationships, you get lost in someone else's drama, and drama can be exciting. You don't stand on solid ground and never know what's going to happen next. Healthy relationships aren't like this. There is no guesswork and no chasing and no trying to figure out what everything means. Healthy relationships are calm and pleasant. If you've never had a healthy relationship, this can feel really weird at first! Once you realize what's at play and settle into the stability and comfort of a relationship in which your interest is reciprocated, you will realize that it's the most beautiful thing in the world.

Unfortunately, the reason a lot of women can't get a guy to commit is because they discard the ones who are able to give them commitment, and are drawn to the ones that won't or can't. A lot of women also lose out on the chance to have a meaningful relationship because they try to play the game, making a guy "chase," rather than trying to connect in a real way.

## He's Smarter Than He Looks

Here is something I'm sure many of you don't realize. Guys *know* when you're doing things to make them chase you! In order to write about men effectively, I spend a lot of time around men. I can't tell you how many times I've seen my guy friends texting with some girl and then jokingly say, "Now I won't hear back for another two hours, this chick waits at least two hours before answering, I think she sets a timer or something." At first they'll put up with it, but it gets very annoying very fast.

One of my guy friends recently went on two great dates with an awesome girl and in between they've been engaged in the texting dance. She texted him while we were hanging out and he looked at it but didn't respond. I asked him why and he said he couldn't respond right away because the girl never ever does, she always waits a few hours, and he reasoned he would look pathetic if he answered right away. "She's probably just trying to make me want her more," he told me plainly. I asked if it was working and he said not really, it was mostly a nuisance, but he was putting up with it for now because he did genuinely like her. It didn't last long — he gave up on the relationship soon after.

Being too obvious about interest isn't a problem, yet this seems to be what we're all afraid of. We think if we text back right away he'll think we're too eager and he'll be put off. Confident women aren't concerned with this. Think about it, if a woman is secure and confident, she'll see her attraction to a guy as a *good* thing, something he'll find desirable. But if a woman is insecure, she'll see her attraction as something that will turn the guy off, something that needs to be "not obvious" or hidden...

Maybe right now you're thinking: "That can't be right! The chase is important and it's the only way!" Fair enough — there's an element of truth to that. But here's what's really at play. The reason the chase is effective to a certain degree is that it creates a situation where a guy has to work to win you over. Whenever we work for something, we become more invested in it; this is just human nature. However, the work does not need to come through playing a game of cat and mouse. Relationships all come with varying degrees of difficulty, even the best ones. When you can face the challenges head on and overcome them together, you put in the kind of work that gets you to a place of greater connection and a place of deep love and appreciation for one another.

You can find countless books that claim not wanting a guy is what gets you the guy, then tells you how to pretend you don't want him. Pretending you don't want someone is not the same as not wanting something from them and it doesn't matter how clever you think you are, if you're doing something to get what you want, you are in agenda mode, it's obvious, and we've seen how damaging this can be.

I think friendships are a good model of a natural way of relating to someone. When you meet someone new you click with, you don't try to force it to be something; either it develops or it doesn't. If someone comes at you forcefully and is desperate to be your friend, you feel put off by it. And if someone is shady with you, you just don't want to deal with it. When you meet someone new you hit it off with, you don't have a goal in mind; you just let things happen. Try to compare the way you make friends with the way you approach relationships, and see if you spot the differences.

While we're on the subject of chasing, I want to mention that you should never, *ever*, chase after a guy. If he isn't asking you out, just let it go. If he says he doesn't want a relationship, take what he says at face value and move on. As soon as a guy drops the "I don't want a relationship" card, instead of his value instantly going down, which would make sense, his value instantly goes up in a woman's eyes. Now he is a challenge, he is the ultimate judge of her worth. If she can prove that she's good enough to be his girlfriend, she will be worthy. If she can't, then she'll have to keep trying until she's finally good enough. The more insecure a girl is, the more

146

entangled she will become in this toxic web. Think of this guy as a drug, and *just say no.*

## Good Relationships Are Effortless

*"The capacity to love is being able to move out of yourself and be with someone else in a manner that is not about your desire to possess them, but to be with them, to be in union and communion."*

*~ Bell Hooks*

Let's talk about what a relationship is and isn't. We'll start with isn't. A relationship isn't a measure of your worth or worthiness in this world. It is not there to serve you and give you things like happiness and self-esteem. It is not there to make you feel good about life and about yourself. This isn't to say a relationship *can't* do these things; it's just that these aren't the elements upon which a healthy relationship is built. A relationship also isn't some sort of milestone, a sign that you have "made it," that you will be okay, that you are now a member of some elite club. It isn't something you work to acquire. It is not a goal to achieve.

A relationship is an experience to be had and shared. It is about discovering how compatible you are with someone, and if there is enough chemistry and compatibility to form a lifelong partnership, often formalized in marriage. The only work you have to do is to make sure you are your best self and get to a place where you can give and receive love. No amount of plotting or analyzing will change whether you and someone else are compatible. You either are or you aren't. Dating is simply a discovery process to find out if you are.

So you enter into the relationship as your best self, and then one of two things happens: It works out or it doesn't. And if it doesn't, you're okay because you know that it just means you weren't a match with that person. It doesn't mean you're flawed or damaged or bad or unlovable. It just wasn't a match. Sometimes you'll be able to see this, sometimes the other person will have that clarity. Either way, if it doesn't work it's because it wasn't the right fit. That's all!

In the right relationship, you don't feel like you're walking on eggshells, worrying that you might screw something up. You don't feel like you have to *make it work*. You don't feel like you're suffocating, wishing and hoping you'll finally get some sweet relief and be able to breathe again. You aren't afraid of losing him. In fact, you never even think about the possibility of losing him, because you don't feel you need to possess him in order to experience the love you have for him.

You can't look at relationships like they'll complete you, be your salvation, make you happy, or make life better. When you start placing these expectations on what a relationship will bring you, you are no longer in the present, you are engaging in a perceived better and brighter future, a fantasy future. When women create this fantasy future, they go blind to what's in front of them.

In a good relationship, both people are happy with their own lives and bring a sense of fulfillment to the relationship, giving and sharing and receiving of each other's fullness. A dysfunctional relationship is when one or both people believe the other person can or should "give them" something, or that there's something to "get" from the other person. This flawed quid-pro-quo mindset will create a relationship dynamic where one or both people suck each other dry. At best, they will have a short-term codependent relationship… which will end once one or both of them are sucked dry, or when one person recognizes there is nothing to be "gotten" from the other person, either because they believe that person can't give it to them or because they reach the deeper understanding that no one can "give them" anything.

148

# When a Guy Wants to Commit to You, He Will Commit to You

There are times when a guy really likes you, but not enough to commit to you. This usually has to do with him, not you. And that's fine. I'm sure you've known some great, attractive, wonderful guys you loved spending time with but didn't have the sorts of feelings necessary for a serious relationship to develop.

## Personal Story

I met a guy a while back and felt an instant and immediate connection. He had the sort of charisma that I'm always drawn to and the vibe between us felt easy and effortless. I was ecstatic when he asked me out, and our first date was amazing. I think it was made more amazing because I had recently been on a string of horrendous dates and was at that terrifying point where I started to truly believe there was not one single man out there for me. This one gave me hope, and it was a glorious feeling.

After only a few dates though, he abruptly pulled the plug. He called me up one day and told me straight out that while he liked me very much, he just didn't see it working out between us long term. I was shocked and devastated. I literally felt as though I had been knocked off balance, to the point where I found it difficult to even walk in a straight line the next day. I spent a solid month trying to understand what went wrong, why it ended so abruptly, and what I possibly could have done differently.

The obsessing didn't get me anywhere (not surprisingly) and after maybe another month the ruminating had run its course and I was starting to get back to a positive place... and then I ran into him at a party. Fueled by too much tequila, I asked him straight up why he'd ended it before it even really got started. I knew it had to be something about me — maybe he wasn't attracted to me, maybe I talked too much, maybe I showed signs of insecurity… it had to be something concrete and tangible!

It wasn't, though. He said he just had a feeling. He just knew I wasn't the girl he was going to end up with, and he didn't want to waste my time. I appreciated that to an extent, but even still, the chemistry between us was electric and I believed it had to mean something. We talked for a while, which led to intense making out, which led to staying up all night and talking, *really talking*, about everything. It was the kind of intimate conversation that makes you feel seen and understood. He liked me, I knew he liked me. He *obviously* liked me. But nothing came of it.

We ran into each other several other times over the course of a few months and it was always the same. Great conversation, intense connection, passion… then nothing.

It took me a long time, way longer that it should have, to realize that while he did like me, while he was attracted to me, while he did find me interesting and fun and cool, he just didn't want to be with me. I could sit and analyze the signs all day long, but it didn't change the reality of the situation. Maybe it was something about me, maybe it was the result of issues he needed to deal with in himself, it didn't matter. The reasons never matter, the facts do.

And with that realization I, at long last, untethered myself from the situation and was able to move on. And in time I realized he was totally right, it never ever would have worked out between us, and he is so not he kind of guy I need. Looking back, the only question I have left is: What in the world was I thinking?!

---

**Does he really love me?**

**Take the QUIZ and find out:**
**www.anewmode.com/love-me-quiz**

---

## When a Guy Says He Doesn't Want a Relationship with You... Believe Him

*"Loving someone who doesn't love you is like waiting for a ship at the airport."*

*~ Unknown*

The mistake I made in the story above is that even though he told me he didn't want a relationship with me, I didn't believe him. Instead, I convinced myself if only we spent more time together, if only he got to know me a little better, if only I gave it more time ... *then* it would all work out. This line of thinking was a huge mistake that cost me almost a year of my dating life. A year spent clinging to hope and ignoring the straightforward facts. With men, it's never all that complicated. When he says he doesn't want a relationship with you, he means it. The reasons don't matter. Maybe it's something specific about you, maybe it's just a gut feeling. There will be times when you'll be the one with the clarity to recognize a relationship isn't right and will have to hurt a guy who believes otherwise, and times when the guy will have the clarity and you'll be thrown off-kilter. It's not always fair, and sometimes it can really hurt... but it's just the nature of the game.

Not everyone is a match for everyone else. For instance, one of my guy friends was dating a beautiful, charming, charismatic, all

151

around awesome girl, but he refused to be exclusive with her. She was understandably annoyed and upset and eventually it ended. I asked him why he wouldn't just commit to her — she was awesome! He told me that while he thought the world of her and really wanted it to work out, he just felt she was too immature and he really had trouble with her way of communicating and dealing with conflict. When issues would come up, she would ignore his calls and texts (or send cold, one-word answers) while he would try and try to talk about it and resolve the problem. On top of that, he felt there was a personality clash; her super energetic disposition, while very fun to be around, could be draining to him at times. There will be many guys who find her energy irresistible, but he didn't. It didn't mean there was something wrong with her, she just wasn't right for *him*.

The reason I wanted to share that story is because I'm hoping you'll realize something I wish I had when I was younger: It's not personal. A guy not wanting to be with you doesn't mean you're defective or unlovable or not good enough, it just means you're not right for him.

In relationships, we all have what we want to give and get. If what you give is what the other person wants to get and vice versa, it's a match! If not, then it's not. If we could just remove our egos and emotions from these situations, and see a relationship for what it is, we would all fare a lot better. You can't fake chemistry or compatibility. They either exist or they don't. You can try to fake or create these things, but the jig will be up at some point, and then what? Also, the amount of energy required to fake something that occurs so easily and effortlessly in the right relationship is unnecessary and exhausting.

You need to find someone who likes the entire picture, not just pieces of you. You can't hide who you are forever... you'll drain all your energy trying to portray yourself as someone you're not, and

152

your real self will always come out in the end. If he doesn't like and accept you for who you really are, how can you expect to ever have a happy relationship with him? If you show who you really are and he leaves, it means it was never going to work. And that's not a loss. Don't blame yourself for what you did wrong, because it never would have worked. You lost nothing. All that happened is you discovered you were incompatible.

Don't cling to hope, don't try to read between the lines, and don't try to shove a square peg into a round hole. If he tells you he doesn't want to be in a relationship, believe him and move on. The sooner you do, the sooner you will find a man who can give you everything you want.

## What Every Guy Likes in a Girl

*"Far too many people are looking for the right person instead of trying to be the right person."*

*~ Gloria Steinem*

Ask ten women what they want in a guy and you'll get ten different answers. For guys, it comes down to one main thing: guys want a woman who will be in their corner and make their lives a better place. If you are pleasant and enjoyable to be around, if you love your life and let that *joie de vivre* flow into your relationship, if you are happy with who he is, then he will be drawn to you like the proverbial moth to a flame.

There is so much information out there about what guys want and how to catch a man, but *that* is what it actually takes. It's not about playing coy or being unattainable or making him chase you or wearing this and saying that. Attracting the *right* man and being in the right relationship comes down to being your best self and letting that flow into the relationship.

Of course, we can't discount the importance of physical attraction and compatibility. Those are prerequisites; if you don't have them, it won't go anywhere. But that aside, it comes down to being the woman who "gets" him, who is his sanctuary, his escape from the world. That is really all any man wants from a woman and from a relationship; everything else is just icing on the cake.

## How Men Commit

What you need to realize about men is they don't really think about commitment until they have to. They enter into a situation and it feels nice, and the commitment just kind of happens. It's not the goal, it's the result.

Here is how commitment usually unfolds from a man's point of view.

A guy meets a girl, and they exchange information, maybe they even hook up. They communicate and start hanging out, and he notices he enjoys spending time with her... and he actually really enjoys her as a person. He realizes that he would even like spending time with her if they didn't hook up.

He feels like his life is better with her around. She doesn't try to capture him or pin him down, and she genuinely enjoys his company as well. He doesn't think about how he'll feel down the line, he just considers how he feels right now, and right now, he feels great. Guys don't think about emotions; if it feels good when she's around, he'll want to be around her.

Guys commit slowly. He doesn't think about it really, he just thinks about how much he enjoys her company, and the fact that he would like more of it. The reason women struggle is because they get an idea in their head that things are not okay. The moment they start to really believe that, they feel uneasy without knowing exactly why.

154

And it doesn't feel good... it makes her feel like she has to do something to feel okay again. Preconceived expectations and conditions can ruin happiness. As soon as they come into play, the nice, ready, relaxed dynamic is ruined. This is when a guy will start to have doubts, when he'll start to pull away, when he'll feel like the walls are closing in and he needs to escape.

Ultimately, a man doesn't consciously choose to commit... it just sort of happens the moment he realizes that this relationship and this woman fulfill him in ways that being single and free never could.

Another key component of commitment is timing. For a man to commit, it has to be the right girl and the right time, and these two things don't always converge. A guy can be dating the right girl, but it just isn't the right time for him to take whatever the next step is that she wants to take; usually this happens with getting engaged or married. I know guys who were sure their girlfriend was "the one," but they didn't want to propose until they were more financially stable or more established in their job. I also know guys who felt ready to find the one and settle down, but it took time to find the right girl. Some guys have such a strong desire to get married (I see this a lot with my single guy friends over 35), that they will try with all their might to make a relationship that wouldn't have gone beyond two dates in the past turn into a marriage. And finally, when a guy is ready to settle down and meets the right girl, *then* it's magic. Then you have that seamless coming together, that instant click and realization that *this is it.*

## Make This Your Mantra

- Commitment for a man comes down to one question: Is my life better with her in it or not?
- The chase creates the illusion of chemistry, not a real connection. A man can sense when you're making him chase

you, and if you keep it up you'll succeed in one thing: chasing him away.

- A relationship isn't a goal or a possession. It is an experience to be had and shared. It is about discovering how compatible you are with someone else, and if there is enough chemistry and compatibility to form a lifelong partnership.
- When a guy says he doesn't want to be in a relationship with you, believe him and don't take it personally.
- A man doesn't consciously choose to commit... it just sort of happens the moment he realizes that this relationship and this woman fulfill him in ways that being single and free never could.

## Exercise

If you're in the dating market, try to abandon your beliefs about needing to make men chase you, and instead try to just be your authentic self. Consider this:

- How do you feel when you have to chase someone in order to keep him?
- How would you feel if someone were deliberately making you feel like you had to chase him?
- How do you feel when you like a guy and don't know how he feels about you?
- How do you feel when you can't tell if he's holding back intentionally, or if he just isn't all that interested?

# Resources

Check out the Chapter 9 resource section (www.anewmode.com/resource) to learn more about how men approach commitment, the qualities that make him *want* to commit, and more.

Articles include:

Ask a Guy: Do Guys Really Love the Chase?

5 Signs He's Not "The One"

How to Have "The Talk" to Define Your Relationship

Ask a Guy: Is There a Chance He Will Finally Commit?

4 Ways to Make Him Commit and Want Only You

Ask a Guy: How Can I Make My Relationship Last?

# Chapter 10: Men Are Not Intentionally Trying to Hurt You

*"We are all here for some special reason. Stop being a prisoner of your past. Become the architect of your future."*

~ *Robin Sharma*

One of the biggest hurdles women trying to find lasting love face exists in their own minds. It's their ingrained belief that men are lying jerks, that they will break your heart, that they're bad, that all the good ones are taken, that all they want is sex. I get it. I have had my heart torn to shreds, leaving me feeling like a hopeless victim and desperately trying to understand *why*. Why are men so cruel? Why do they lie? Why do they disappear? Why are they so selfish?

This whole man versus woman mentality is absolute poison when it comes to getting the love you want. The risk we take when opening our hearts and choosing to love is the risk of being hurt. As they say… the bigger the risk, the bigger the reward. Some men will hurt you, some will shatter your heart, some will betray your trust, but the majority of the time when this happens, it wasn't intentional. If you internalize the pain and punish your new guy for the last guy's mistakes, you will never be free and you will never find happiness or satisfaction in your relationship. At the end of the day, holding onto these feelings and past pains will not serve you in any positive way.

## When You Know the Truth…

You will realize that blaming and hating men is only hurting you. You will realize that like us, men also have flaws and insecurities and vulnerabilities, and sometimes they manifest in hurtful ways.

It's not intentional (unless the guy is a total sociopath), and it doesn't say anything about you.

When you can step outside of yourself and see the world with someone else's perspective, you will understand that it isn't personal... it's just life. You will free yourself from debilitating beliefs that cause you to transmit a negative, off-putting vibe that men pick up on, and instead will radiate warmth and openness. You will stop being a victim of other people and circumstance, and will have control over your life and, at long last, get the love you've always wanted.

## Men Are Not the Bad Guys

*"Holding on to anger is like grasping a hot coal
with the intent of throwing it at someone else; you
are the one getting burned."*

*~ Buddha*

In order to be happy and find lasting love, you must free yourself from the idea that men are bad, evil, commitment-phobic jerks who will break your heart. For one thing, this isn't true of most men. Maybe it's true of some men, but not most. Also, holding onto this idea creates a vibe and an energy that will push men away. Negative thoughts never bring joy or resolution, they only make life more painful for you.

Think of it this way, would you want to date a guy who thought all women were manipulative, gold-digging bitches? No. So why would a guy want to date a girl with similarly negative sentiments against all men? Just like women can intuitively pick up on a man being chauvinistic, men can sense when a woman is a man-hater. This doesn't just apply to single girls, women in relationships can also fall into man-hating thought patterns.

I have a guy friend who is the ultimate validation for women. He is incredibly good-looking and charismatic, and his combination of looks and confidence makes it easy for him to get any girl he wants. Being chosen by a man who has tons of choices is incredibly validating. Every woman knows that feeling, and even I'll admit it can make you feel really special. Who doesn't want that? A little while ago he met a girl who totally blew him away. She was gorgeous, cool, fun, and really smart. After their first conversation she said: "Whatever you do, don't fall in love with me," which he found really cute. He liked her easy vibe and didn't feel any pressure coming from her. He responded to her warning by saying she would "eat her words" in a few weeks. She laughed at the time, but his prophecy quickly came true.

Soon and suddenly everything shifted. He did as she asked and didn't fall in love with her, but she fell very much in love with him. He was well on his way to developing real feelings for her, but it was way too soon and he was taken aback by it given her "don't fall in love with me" comment and the fact that the relationship was only a few weeks old. Every time they hung out, she would ask him how he felt about her, she would complain he wasn't being affectionate enough, and she would often say she couldn't "feel his emotions" when they were being intimate. He tried to just go with it, but told me the pressure just became too much. She always wanted more and would end up screaming at him and crying and sending him angry texts about what a bastard he was. He was really disappointed by the entire thing and pretty confused, too. He didn't understand how a girl who seemed so confident could become so needy, or why she presented herself as being a certain kind of girl when she clearly wasn't.

The sad fact is that this girl did what many of us do. She attached her sense of self-worth to the status of her relationship. She didn't have a strong enough self-esteem to believe such a desirable guy could want her, so she was always questioning it and emotionally

160

reacting to any small thing he did. Yet instead of looking within and seeing that she was the root cause of the problems she was experiencing with this guy, she blamed him, made him the bad guy, called him a bastard. But he was not the bad guy — nothing he did would have given her the validation she needed.

Remember, this line of thinking — blaming men — doesn't serve you; it only hurts you and blocks you from getting what you really want. Men don't normally have bad intentions, often they do things because they don't *want* to hurt you.

For instance, I've asked many guys why they simply ghost instead of telling a girl to her face they do not want to continue the relationship. I've been on the receiving end of this, and it sucks and seems cowardly on the guy's part. Across the board, guys have told me they just don't want to be the one to hurt a girl or make her upset. No guy wants to feel like that. Instead, he prefers to think that maybe you and he are on the same page... maybe you also realized it wasn't working, and calling and telling you that would just be presumptuous. He doesn't ghost because he wants to hurt you; in fact, he prefers to just think that you are totally fine, that you are doing your thing and are totally okay. Calling you up and hearing how hurt you are would be tough for him, and men aren't always very good at handling uncomfortable emotional situations. It doesn't make it right, but it does make sense.

I get really frustrated when I hear women say things like, "All the good men are taken," "Men are all scumbags," "Men are lying cheaters," because... really? *All men?* This is just a ridiculous blanket statement, and it isn't true.

A lot of women also get frustrated because they feel like men don't have to do anything, and the woman is the one who has to make the relationship work, or mold her behavior. This isn't true either. Men also want to have good, positive relationships. And there are many

161

websites dedicated to giving relationship advice to men. At the same time, women are naturally better at building relationships. And usually, when a woman is in a good place and is her best self, the man rises up and becomes his best self as well.

The only person you can change is yourself. You can't ever force someone else to change. You can inspire him to be better, but you can't do the work for him. All you can do is work on improving yourself. If a guy works well with you, it's a match. If not, you will be free to move on to something better.

## Eric Confession

"I'll admit I've done the fade-away on girls I was no longer interested in. I just assume the girl knows she'll hear from me if I want to see her more. I just listen to my "wanting"... if I'm not into it, if I don't feel a desire to reach out to her or see her, I'm done. Guys know girls only get more and more attached, so if we're not feeling it, we just stop reaching out. I just assume she feels the same way as far as not really being into it, and if she doesn't, well, then we're not a good match because we're not on the same page ... and that's how I can sleep at night."

## Is it Him or Is It You?

*"A positive attitude gives you power over your circumstances instead of your circumstances having power over you."*

~ *Joyce Meyer*

If every guy you have ever dated has treated you poorly and broken your heart, then you need to consider that you are probably choosing the wrong men. If you stay with a guy even though he has made it clear he can't or won't give you what you want, and the relationship deteriorates, you can't exactly blame him. It's much easier to point the finger at someone else when we feel hurt, but there comes a point when we need to learn to take responsibility for our own happiness.

When a woman believes a guy will give her the validation she wants or needs, she may put up with a lot of bad behavior in order to get it. Even if the relationship isn't a particularly good one, she will strategize and plot ways to earn his love, believing this will grant her relief from whatever inner suffering she is feeling.

When a relationship ends and you feel betrayed or hurt, it's a lot easier to pin it on external sources than to fix the internal issues that may have caused you to get into, and stay in, a situation you knew wasn't healthy.

Your time is *your* responsibility. No one can make you do anything unless they're holding a gun to your head. You stayed because you were getting something out of the situation, just like he was. The worst thing you can do to yourself is hold onto bitterness and rage. These feelings may be understandable, but they won't serve any positive function, they will just make you hardened, angry, and jaded, all of which will block you from meeting someone who can actually give you the relationship you want.

## Personal Story

In the beginning of my relationship with my husband, insecurities flared up because of unresolved pain. I had a really hard time trusting him and the relationship in the beginning, but it had absolutely nothing to do with him, it was all me. He was nothing but kind and open and honest and loving from day one. But I noticed that certain innocent things were triggers for me…

When my insecurities would flare up, he would say "I'm not going

163

anywhere," and he meant it. But any time he would say those words, I would feel my guard reflexively come up. With a little self-reflection I was able to pinpoint exactly why it was happening.

You see, a former boyfriend used to say the same thing. In that relationship, my insecurities had a clear source: He refused to call me his girlfriend. Any time I needed to be reassured, he would tell me he wasn't going anywhere, and I would feel calm and secure. Those words would soothe me, and they even convinced me to ignore the fact that he refused to commit in a real way. Even though the relationship was far from ideal, I truly believed him when he said he would never leave. I believed he couldn't live without me, just as I couldn't possibly fathom a world without him. But he did leave me. He left me for somebody else, and from that moment on I stopped trusting myself and I stopped trusting men. I internalized a belief that I was unworthy of love, that any guy I gave my heart to wouldn't love me back, and I didn't really challenge this belief until my current guy came along. Love tends to bring up all that is unloved within us.

Even though I had done a lot of internal work before I started dating my current guy, there was a lot more that needed to be done. It started with realizing that this relationship is the complete opposite of the last one, and I am a completely different person now, so it is absurd to think I would repeat the same mistakes. But our subconscious doesn't operate from a place of reason and logic, it operates from emotion. What I needed to realize was that even though certain things *felt* real (like that he was going to just leave me out of the blue one day and I needed to be on guard at all times, lest I miss some warning sign), that doesn't mean they were reality. Feelings aren't facts, and when you look at a situation objectively you often see just how silly and unfounded your beliefs truly are.

In the same way, just because a guy's behavior is making you feel bad, it doesn't mean he's a bad guy. Sometimes the bad feelings
164

originate in unresolved pain from your past, or feelings of insecurity and fear that have nothing to do with a man being a bad guy and everything to do with you and your own issues.

## Let It Go

*"To be wronged is nothing unless you continue to remember it."*

*~ Confucius*

Put on the *Frozen* soundtrack and give yourself permission to just let go. I'm sure you've been wronged in the past. I've been wronged in the past, too. But it does you no good to hold onto this pain, and really, you're only hurting yourself. Give yourself permission to forgive and move on. Maybe he doesn't deserve your forgiveness, but so what? He also doesn't deserve to have power over your mood and your ability to give and receive love.

Time does heal in a way, but not on its own. Time merely rearranges our memories. It moves certain things to the background, where they can't be readily accessed but can still be felt, sometimes slightly and sometimes more intensely. It is up to you to heal from whatever broke you. Don't escape the pain or wait it out. Look it in the face, confront it, then release it.

## Make This Your Mantra

- Thinking all men are evil is poisonous and can block you from ever having the love you want.
- Men don't have bad intentions; often they do things because they don't want to hurt you.
- When a relationship ends and you feel betrayed or hurt, it's a lot easier to pin it on external sources than to fix the internal issues

that may have caused you to get into, and stay in, a situation you knew wasn't healthy.

- Your time is your responsibility. If you stayed in a bad relationship and it didn't turn out well, you are partly to blame.
- Learn to let go, forgive, and move on. Make this a priority — do whatever it takes to get there.

# Exercise

- Visualize yourself forgiving a guy who has wronged you. Paint the scene in your mind: Look at him and say you forgive him for everything. Then wish him the best and really try to force yourself to mean it and feel those positive sentiments flowing through you. Repeat as necessary for all the guys who have wronged you, until you're able to let go of the pain and move on.
- Write a letter that you don't send. Just write it all out, everything you're thinking and feeling. Sometimes you won't even know how you really feel and what hurt the most until you put pen to paper.

# Resources

From lying to pulling a disappearing act, find out the real reason guys do these hurtful things and also learn how to move on from your painful past and into a better future in the resource section for Chapter 10 (www.anewmode.com/resource).

Articles include:

3 Reasons Why You're Still Single

Why Men Lie: The 4 True Reasons

Why Guys Disappear and How to Deal

The Real Reasons You Can't Get Over Him

# Final Thoughts

*"No one can go back and make a brand new start,*
*my friend, but anyone can start from here and make*
*a brand new end."*

*~ Dan Zadra*

So here we are, we've made it to the end and are hopefully ready to embark on a new beginning. It took me a long time to realize all the truths I shared in this book. There are different levels of knowing something: You can hear something and acknowledge it as truth, but it's only when you live it and experience it that you can grasp what it truly means and internalize it.

At the end of the day, a relationship is a partnership. It's about coming together in unity and harmony and working together to create something long-lasting and meaningful. When done right, a relationship can help you become your best self, it can encourage you to grow and heal and tap into parts of yourself that you didn't even know existed. When done wrong, a relationship can destroy you. It can cause scars and pain and leave you confused and unsure of who you are. The pain has a price, but it also has a reward — as long as you can see it as a learning experience and grow from it. I have essentially made a career out of doing just that.

The first step in getting to that place of partnership and being on the same team is to understand where the other side is coming from, and have compassion. Men and women are different. People in general are different. We were all born with a unique set of skills and abilities, we all have been on our own unique journeys, we all face a certain degree of adversity. But we can still learn to see beyond our own experiences and gain an understanding of someone else's.

When you don't understand men, they can seem like the enemy. Like their sole purpose in life is to leave you hurt and confused. My hope is that this is no longer your line of thinking. I hope you have gained an understanding of how men operate so you don't get sucked into a whirlpool of doubts and insecurities, and can instead reach a place of clarity and confidence.

There are no quick and easy fixes. There is no magic phrase or magic bullet. It takes work, all of it. But it's so rewarding when you get where you need to be. I don't even think I can properly articulate just how rewarding it is to conquer your demons, to heal from your past, to understand what went wrong, and to know that you are better and stronger now than you were then. Even though I write about men and relationships for a living, I still slip up sometimes. Even I find myself getting upset over things I shouldn't. We all bring our baggage into relationships, and we all view life through our own subjective lens.

Heartbreak can be the loneliest feeling. You can seriously feel like the pain is yours alone and no one in the world can ever understand. I used to search desperately for the answers and for someone, anyone, who might understand my pain, or even better, who had been through it and survived! My goal when creating books and articles has always been to write content that I would have found helpful when I needed it. This has been my mission from the beginning, and it never falters.

I hope you take what you've learned and use it to create a happier, brighter future. I hope it leads to lasting love, both with a man and with yourself. And I hope you stay a part of the A New Mode community.

Lots of Love,
Sabrina

# A Note on A New Mode, Eric, and Me

As I mentioned above, a relationship is a partnership — it's about working together to create something long lasting and meaningful. You'll remember that in some of the personal stories I shared in this book, I desperately wanted things to work out with different guys, only to later realize they were completely wrong for me and it never would have worked out. I got so caught up in wanting a certain outcome that I was blind to the present moment and other possibilities. I ended up becoming great friends with some of those guys — that was the right and natural outcome for us, I just couldn't see it at the time. I've since realized that sometimes the thing you're *not* looking for, the outcome you don't expect, well, it can be a beautiful thing.

It was fall, 2008. I had just been laid off and I was devastated. I was working as a fashion and beauty editor for an up-and-coming website, living the kind of fast-paced life that offers little time to come up for air. I'd been wanting to start my own website for a while, but though I was great at talking about it, I didn't actually feel like I knew what I was doing, or how to even get started.

Around this time, the ex-boyfriend who broke my heart in 2006, Eric Charles, came back into my life after years of absolutely no contact. In an attempt to show him how cool and confident I'd become, I shared stories about all the guys who'd been pursuing me, and how desperately they were trying to win me over. I told him my friends had dubbed me the Man-eater. I casually mentioned how much I was getting hit on, how *so* many guys wanted me. I was slightly aware of how pathetic I was being, but I couldn't and wouldn't stop until he realized what a prize I was, what a fool he'd been to let me go!

My efforts didn't have the intended effect; they had a very different one. "You know," he told me. "You should write a book about all

169

this. Write a book that teaches women how to make men worship them, I bet you'd make a fortune."

I felt a bit dejected, but also intrigued.

"Yeah, I could do that. I've always wanted to write a book."

"First you need to create a blog."

"Well I've been wanting to start my own fashion and beauty blog for the past year, but I don't know what I'm doing!"

"Oh, I can do that for you, that's nothing. We'll be partners. You write the content, I'll handle the tech stuff."

"Okay, deal."

And A New Mode was born! It started as a new kind of fashion and beauty site, but I hadn't forgotten my silent vow to create a website designed to empower women, so shortly after we launched, I asked Eric if he'd be up to writing a weekly Ask a Guy column. I knew Eric was the perfect guy to give girls the answers they really needed in a way that was sensitive, yet still honest and insightful. No sugarcoating, no feeding into the fantasies we all create in our heads, no placating people by just telling them what they want to hear. Eric had been researching psychology and relationships for years, and had another business devoted to helping men in relationships. Even though he was supposed to be behind the scenes in this operation, he agreed to take on the role of Ask a Guy…

To kick things off, I had all my girlfriends send him their guy questions. Any time we were out talking about guys and someone had a frustration or complaint, I made them write it down then and there and send it to Eric to publish as an Ask a Guy article. And boy did he deliver! The column was an instant sensation, and we were soon getting flooded with questions via e-mail. It was the life-changing turning point I knew it would be.

Every week I would pick out the best question from the bunch and have Eric answer. Then I would edit and publish it. The articles were always intensely eye-opening for me. Sometimes I had a hard time believing the things he was saying and would think, "Okay, maybe Eric feels this way, but there's no way that's true of *all* men."

But a funny thing started to happen. When I went out on dates, I started taking notice of things that I normally would have ignored or written off or rationalized. I started to spot the behaviors and nuances that Eric was talking about... and I understood what they meant. I understood men! It was amazing and liberating, and I just couldn't believe how much I simply had not known about this not-so-mysterious gender. I quickly became a go-to advice girl for my friends when it came to their guy problems. And they were stunned by how unambiguously I could explain their situation and what the guy was thinking. I could even predict with precise accuracy how relationships would unfold. What he would do... what he would say... when he would text back. My friends referred to it as my Spidey Sense.

In fall 2011, after years spent researching relationships, studying human behavior, and being a free relationship coach to basically everyone I knew, I finally felt confident enough to write about relationships on A New Mode. Up until then, I had handled all the other sections, but as the site moved away from fashion and beauty and became completely relationship focused, I knew it was time to share my voice... I just hoped everyone would take me seriously.

Eric naturally has insights into the male mind that I can never possess. I didn't aim to explain men the way he did, because that

171

just wasn't possible. Instead, I started sharing my own stories and experiences. I used the insights Eric shared each week to illustrate how these concepts had played out in my dating life and in the lives of my friends, who kindly let me write about their experiences. And to my huge relief, it was a hit. Our readers loved what I had to say. They really connected to my experiences and found value in the lessons I had learned. I hoped they felt the same bond with me that I'd felt with Jennifer Aniston when I read how she got through her painful breakup — a sense of sisterhood and renewed hope from knowing that someone who had gone through the same kind of pain was able to come out on the other side, and to do so with clarity and a deeper understanding of men and relationship dynamics in general.

I've always been the type of person who needs to understand everything about everything. If something piques my interest, I become insatiably driven to know absolutely everything there is to know about it. Human beings are complex and relationship dynamics can be tricky, but I have observed certain universal truths that apply across almost all ages and cultures.

More importantly, I've lived it. I've been there. I've been hurt, I've been defeated. I've felt hopeless and so utterly confused. I know what it is to have your sense of worth tightly clenched in a man's unrelenting grip. I know the extreme high of feeling worthy and okay when he approves... and the devastating anguish of feeling like I will never quite measure up when he doesn't. I know the fear that you'll never be worthy of getting the love you want. And I know how to write about it, to help you learn from my experiences.

A New Mode currently clocks in over 10 million visitors annually from women all over the world looking to understand men and get the love and relationships they've always wanted. We wrote an e-book called *He's Not That Complicated* (available at www.anewmode.com/hntc) that has sold tens of thousands of copies. We created an audio series, a newsletter with half a million subscribers, a quiz section (www.anewmode.com/quizzes), and tons and tons of content devoted to uncovering the truth about relationships.

Writing about relationships on A New Mode is now what I do full time, and it isn't just a job for me, it's almost like therapy. In writing about relationships, I've been able to identify my own faulty patterns and correct them, and it has helped me grow enormously. And it's pretty cool to see our readers grow along with me.

A New Mode is more than a content site, it is a community. I hope you will check out the site (www.anewmode.com) and participate in the forum whenever you find yourself struggling or think you can help someone else who needs advice.

## Stay in touch!

If you have thoughts/feedback/comments, don't be a stranger, shoot me an e-mail - sabrina@anewmode.com.

You can also find A New Mode on …

**Facebook: facebook.com/anmdaily**

**Twitter: @anewmode**

**Instagram: instagram.com/anewmode**

**Pinterest: pinterest.com/anewmode**

Also!

Join our newsletter for personal, original content written by Eric and me on a variety of relationship topics - www.anewmode.com/subscribe

# Acknowledgments

I want to give a special thank-you to Loreen Thompson, who went above and beyond the call of duty as an editor, giving me invaluable feedback and suggestions along the way that made the book more cohesive and got the message across even stronger.

Thank you to Asia Williams for creating another brilliant book cover for us (and for making all the amazing collage images on A New Mode).

To my friends, who are gracious enough to allow me to use their tales of love gone wrong to help others. Thank you for not only providing me with endless material, but also with endless love and support.

Thank you to my parents, who always supported me no matter what and couldn't be more proud of their daughter, the writer.

To our readers, for being so supportive of the work we do. Thank you for sharing your souls, for pouring your hearts out, for asking your questions, for leaving your feedback, and for sharing your triumphs and also your heartaches. (Our hope is that this book will make the heartaches less frequent!) You guys are awesome and we're so lucky to have you as a part of the ANM community.

Thank you to Eric, my friend and business partner, for believing in my writing abilities and in my insights and for pushing me past my fears and self-doubts all those years ago and encouraging me to start ANM... and later pushing me to start writing about relationships even though I wanted to remain behind the safe confines of being a fashion and beauty writer... and later for pushing me to write our first book, *He's Not That Complicated*, and not letting me weasel out of it even though the thought of writing a book was daunting and terrifying to me. I would never have found the strength to do it on my own, and now writing about relationships is the thing I love doing more than anything else. While like any partnership it's challenging at times, the rewards more than make up for it and ANM wouldn't exist without Eric's determination and vision. Without him, I (along with countless other women out there) would probably still be mostly clueless about men, and for that I am eternally grateful.

And last but most certainly not least, to my amazing husband, my partner in everything and the love of my life. If I said how I really feel it would make everyone gag from cheesiness, so I'll spare you the sappiness, but thank you for being my number one fan, my biggest supporter, and for ultimately giving me the kind of love that I spent years writing about as a single girl, the kind of love that I sometimes wasn't sure even existed, the kind of love that made all the painful experiences I went through so worth it. You are everything.

Printed in Great Britain
by Amazon